Future Application and Middleware Technology on e-Science

Ok-Hwan Byeon • Jang Hyuk Kwon • Thom Dunning
Kum Won Cho • Aurore Savoy-Navarro
Editors

Future Application and Middleware Technology on e-Science

Springer

Editors
Ok-Hwan Byeon
Korea Institute of Science and
Technology Information (KISTI)
335 Gwahangno
Daejeon 305-806
Yusung-gu
Republic of Korea
ohbyeon@kisti.re.kr

Jang Hyuk Kwon
Department of Aerospace Engineering
Korea Advanced Institute of Science
and Technology (KAIST)
373-1 Guseong-dong
Daejeon 305-701
Yuseong-gu
Republic of Korea
jhkwon@kaist.ac.kr

Thom Dunning
National Center for Supercomputing
Application(NCSA)
1205 W. Clark Street
Urbana, IL 61801
USA

Kum Won Cho
Korea Institute of Science and
Technology Information (KISTI)
335 Gwahangno
Daejeon 305-806
Yusung-gu
Republic of Korea
ckw@kisti.re.kr

Aurore Savoy-Navarro
Université Paris VI
Labo. Physique Nucléaire et de
Hautes Energies (LPNHE)
4 Place Jussieu
75252 Paris CX5
France

ISBN 978-1-4899-8526-2 ISBN 978-1-4419-1719-5 (eBook)
DOI 10.1007/978-1-4419-1719-5
Springer New York Dordrecht Heidelberg London

Printed on acid-free paper

Springer is part of Springer Science+Business Media (www.springer.com)

Contents

Web-Based Integrated Research Environment for Aerodynamic Analyses and Design

Jae Wan Ahn[*], Jin-ho Kim[*], Chongam Kim[*], Jung-hyun Cho[†], Cinyoung Hur[†], Yoonhee Kim[†], Sang-hyun Kang[‡], Byungsoo Kim[‡], Jong Bae Moon[§], and Kum Won Cho[§]

[*]School of Mechanical and Aerospace Eng. Seoul National Univ.
{ajw158, keias21, chongam}@snu.ac.kr

[†]Dept. of Computer Science, Sookmyung Women's Univ.
{abaekho, hurcy, yulan}@sm.ac.kr

[‡]Dept. of Aerospace Eng. Chungnam National Univ.
norynory@hanmail.net, kbskbs@cnu.ac.kr

[§]e-Science Application Research Team, KISTI
{jbmoon, ckw}@kisti.re.kr

Abstract e-AIRS[1,2], an abbreviation of 'e-Science Aerospace Integrated Research System,' is a virtual organization designed to support aerodynamic flow analyses in aerospace engineering using the e-Science environment. As the first step toward a virtual aerospace engineering organization, e-AIRS intends to give a full support of aerodynamic research process. Currently, e-AIRS can handle both the computational and experimental aerodynamic research on the e-Science infrastructure. In detail, users can conduct a full CFD (Computational Fluid Dynamics) research process, request wind tunnel experiment, perform comparative analysis between computational prediction and experimental measurement, and finally, collaborate with other researchers using the web portal. The present paper describes those services and the internal architecture of the e-AIRS system.

1 Introduction

Aerospace engineering research is a system-intensive activity. The design of aerospace products requires cooperative and integrated researches among various disciplines, such as aerodynamics, structure, propulsion, and control. Thus, an aerospace engineering environment should offer both sufficient research space to

O.-H. Byeon et al. (eds.), *Future Application and Middleware Technology on e-Science*, DOI 10.1007/978-1-4419-1719-5_1, © Springer Science+Business Media, LLC 2010

each discipline and a convenient collaboration system. Here, a sufficient research space means an adequate supply of research equipments, such as computing resources or experimental facilities. The research space should include software optimized for specific research field. On the other hand, a convenient collaboration system needs to be more general-purpose, i.e., applicable to various disciplines. A collaboration system plays the role of controlling the connection among researchers, giving a secure space for remote discussion and supporting visualization routine.

From this point of view, the e-Science[3] environment can be an ideal answer in constructing an integrated research environment for aerospace engineering. For specific research, the Grid computing technology[4,5], with high-speed networks and various middleware, supports the resource pool of cluster computers, personal computers, experimental equipment, and so on. Application-oriented tools, such as flow analysis and visualization software, can be developed and included in a system through the collaboration between application researchers and computer scientists. Then, human resources can interact with the system via an on-line portal. Inter-disciplinary collaboration can be achieved by using supporting software such as the AGTk (Access Grid Toolkit)[6] and by developing some additional plug-ins for an application target.

In other words, a user-friendly interface is an important factor in the e-Science environment. If users can access the research system using the Internet portal through user-friendly GUI, researchers can be able to carry out their on-going research activities regardless of time and location.

The present study focuses on developing a virtual organization infrastructure for aerospace engineering, and then applying it to aerodynamic research process. The current system, called e-AIRS, covers component research modules of computational and experimental aerodynamics, along with the integration of those two research activities and the remote discussion between computational and experimental researchers. The key characteristics and features of e-AIRS are described in the following sections.

2 Backgrounds and Strategy

The Korean e-Science research project has been launched since 2005 with the support from the Korean Ministry of Science and Technology. On the basis of the Korean Grid infrastructure, which is the product of the Korean Grid research project, five research topics were selected as killer applications. They include the remote imaging service of an electron microscope, climate information system, molecular simulation, bioinformatics, and the present integrated aerodynamic research system.

As an e-Science environment for aerospace engineering, e-AIRS has referred to some of the previous research projects carried out on international scale. As the representative e-Science research in aerospace technology, a few projects in the

UK e-Science program can be considered. Those are DAME (A Distributed Aircraft engine Maintenance Environment)[7,8], GEODISE (Grid-Enabled Optimisation and Design Search for Engineering)[9], GECEM (Grid-Enabled Computational Electromagnetics)[10], and GEWiTTS (Grid-Enabled Wind Tunnel Test System)[11]. These works can be evaluated as pioneering researches in the application of e-Science to aerospace technology, and they depicted the blueprint of scientific and engineering infrastructure standard. Additionally, the TENT, an aerodynamic computing simulation tool[12] in Germany, and the DARWIN, a remote aerospace analysis and knowledge management system[13] in the USA, are good examples of aerospace e-Science environment. However, all of these projects have some weak points in terms of service environment component. For example, they are targeted for professional engineers and only permissible to exclusive members, so that general users can not access or use them. In addition, there is no user-friendly interface or a portal web site for various classes of user groups. Based on the lessons of those studies, e-AIRS has been designed to provide an Internet-based service containing both automatic CFD simulation and remote wind tunnel experiment to general users. The final goal of the e-AIRS research project is to establish a useful virtual research environment that can provide CFD simulation and wind tunnel experiment data.

3 e-AIRS System Overview

The e-AIRS portal (http://eairs.kisti.re.kr/gridsphere/gridsphere) is composed of various portlets, which are developed within the framework of GridSphere[14]. The GridSphere portlet framework provides a solution to construct an open-source web portal. The GridSphere supports standard portlets, and these portlets can be extended to new portlets. The portlets are implemented in Java and can be modified easily.

As mentioned in the previous section, the main goal of e-AIRS is to establish a powerful and user-friendly research environment for aerospace engineering. From this point of view, the e-AIRS portal should provide the main interface through which all of the computational and experimental services can be accessed easily. The portal hides the complexity of the inner system from the end-users. In addition, the portal also provides an interface for various processes required for CFD simulations and remote wind tunnel experiments. This means users can access all of the e-AIRS software and hardware resources through the portal interface. A brief schematic of the e-AIRS portal service is depicted in Figure 1.

As shown in Figure 1, the e-AIRS portal is mainly composed of four sessions: the CFD service, the remote experimental service, the PSS (Parametric Study Service) engine for integrated research, and the collaboration service that links the AGTk. All computational and experimental data are managed in the MMS (Metadata Management System), and those tasks are categorized by adopting the concept of 'Project' and 'Case'. Here, 'Project' means a group of cases and represents an aerodynamic object and 'Case' is a single task with a specific flow property. For example, specific aircraft geometry defines a 'project' and various flow conditions defined by the Mach number and Reynolds number are regared as 'cases'. This hierarch is designed to reflect typical aerodynamic research process, i.e., aerodynamic researchers want to see various flow characteristics for one aerodynamic object geometry.

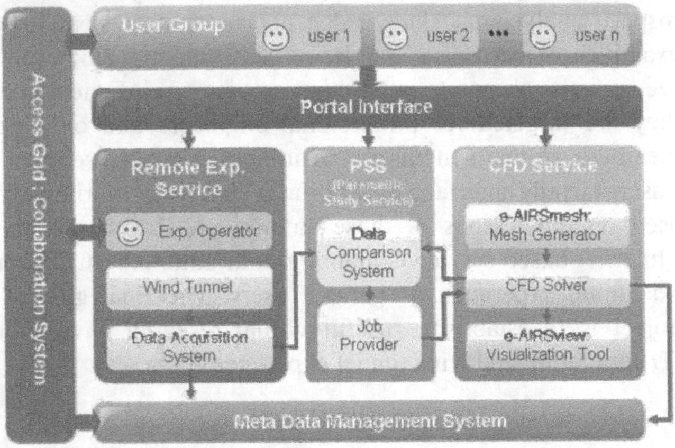

Fig. 1. The schematic of the e-AIRS services

As shown in Fig. 1, every e-AIRS service has its own role for specific research methodology. For example, the PSS service is important in validating computational or experimental results by comparing CFD and experiment data. Based on the comparison, additional flow simulations can be carried out by high throughput computing. This kind of 'research-oriented' service structure is the key originality of the e-AIRS environment.

4 CFD Service

At first, users need to understand a typical CFD (Computational Fluid Dynamics) procedure to numerically analyze an aerodynamic problem. As the fluid dynamics is a scientific discipline which solves flow phenomena around target geometry, constructing the flow computational domain around geometry is the first work. This domain is called 'Mesh.' The domain is composed of many computational cells, and each cell is the unit space to represent the change of flow parameters such as density, velocity, temperature, pressure, and so on. In CFD calculation, a numerical solver provides physical values by computing the governing equations.

General CFD procedures and the relationship between each procedure and each e-AIRS service are depicted in Fig. 2. The mesh generation procedure is carried out by e-AIRSmesh and CAD2MESH software. After the construction of the mesh system, CFD simulation is conducted. The CFD solver is the main part of CFD computation service and it is hidden in the middleware level of the system, because users do not need to know the complex structure or architecture of the simulation code. The CFD solver execution procedure is just matched with CFD execution service and monitoring service. The former is the interface between the computing resources and the user's 'simulation-start' instruction. The latter gives information on the calculations, for examples, current status, convergence history, and so on. Finally, the computational results, which are just tables of numbers, are visualized as figures so that the user can recognize physical characteristics. This visualization or output procedure is accomplished by e-DAVA service.

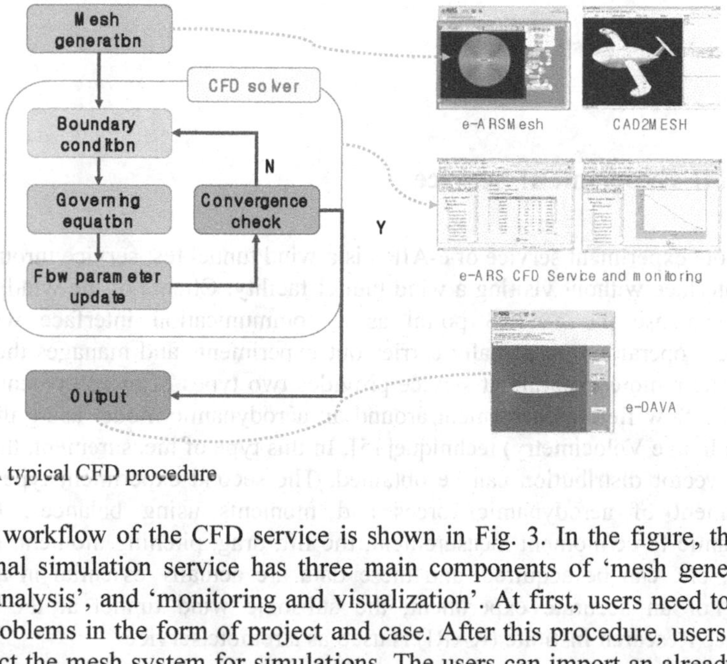

Fig. 2. A typical CFD procedure

The workflow of the CFD service is shown in Fig. 3. In the figure, the computational simulation service has three main components of 'mesh generation', 'CFD analysis', and 'monitoring and visualization'. At first, users need to define their problems in the form of project and case. After this procedure, users should construct the mesh system for simulations. The users can import an already-made mesh file or make a new mesh. To make a new mesh file, the users can access the mesh generation service. In the mesh generation service, the users' input of a CAD data file is converted through CAD2MESH application. The line and surface information about the model geometry is delivered to a mesh generator, e-AIRSmesh. In e-AIRSmesh, users can set up the computational domain around the aerodynamic object, and the mesh data generated is saved in the storage server.

As the second step, users access the CFD solver service and select cases to be simulated. Then, the users' requests are sent to the computing resources, and a simulation automatically starts. During the simulation, the status and residual history of the requested jobs are shown in the monitoring service, and the intermediate and final result data are monitored using the visualization application, e-DAVA.

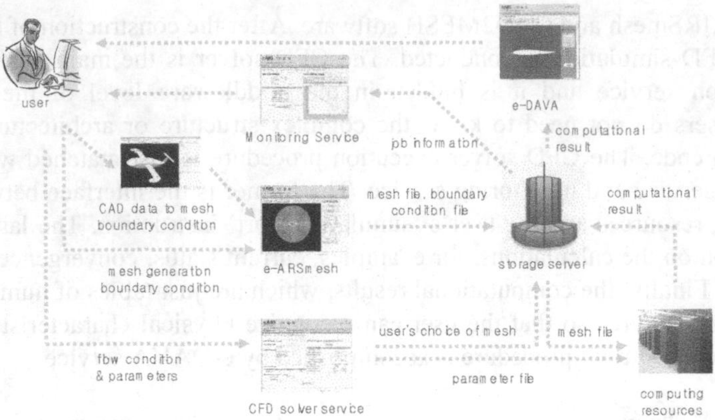

Fig. 3. Overview of the CFD service

5 Remote Experiment Service

The remote experiment service of e-AIRS is a wind tunnel test service through the portal interface without visiting a wind tunnel facility. Clients of the wind tunnel service can use the e-AIRS portal as a communication interface with an experiment operator who actually carries out experiments and manages the wind tunnel. The remote experiment service provides two types of measurements. The first is the flow field measurement around an aerodynamic model using the PIV (Particle Image Velocimetry) technique[15]. In this type of measurement, the flow velocity vector distribution can be obtained. The second experiment type is the measurement of aerodynamic forces and moments using balances. In the aerodynamic force/moment measurement, the lift, drag, pitching moment, rolling moment, etc. can be acquired, and these data are actually essential in aircraft design. For an accurate experiment, the subsonic wind tunnel at the Korea Aerospace Research Institute (KARI) is used as a remote service.

The remote experiment service consists of three services: the experiment request service, the experiment management service, and the experiment information service. A client can request an experiment through the experiment request service. Then the wind tunnel operator checks the newly requested experiments on the experiment management service. The management service offers detailed information about the requested experiment to the operator such as the Reynolds number, the angle of attack, the data form, the test area on the aerodynamic model, and so on. Then the operator can carry out experiments and upload the result data files, including particle images, through the web UI. Finally, a client user can browse and check the status of the experiment through the experiment information service. The states are classified as 'new', 'on-going' and 'finished'. Fig. 4 describes the remote experiment procedures.

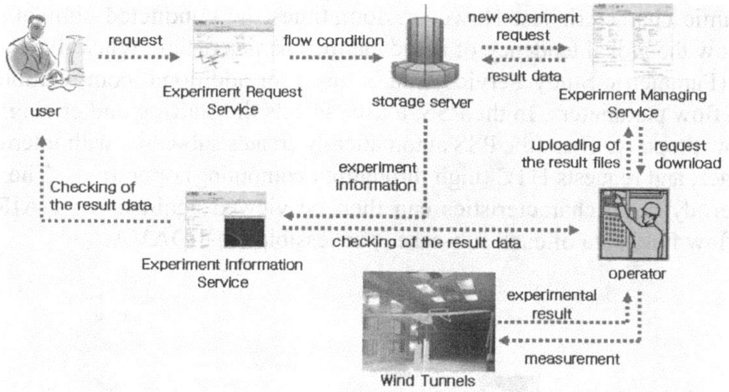

Fig. 4. Overview of the remote experiment service0

6 Integrated Research Support

As mentioned in the introduction, aerodynamic research requires CFD-experiment comparisons. This is very useful in validating either computational or experimental data. Fig. 5 shows this relationship of the data comparison system.

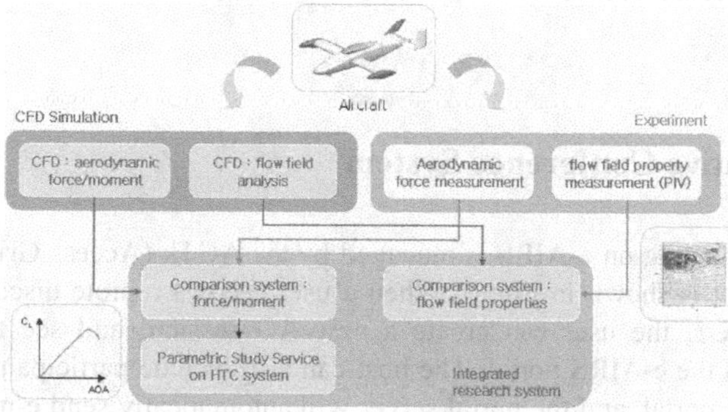

Fig. 5. Integrated research system

Fig. 6 shows the conceptual view of the integrated research support. It firstly starts from individual CFD analyses and experiments conducted beforehand. At first, collected CFD and experimental data in the same project are depicted by a plotting service, called e-AIRSplot. e-AIRSplot plots the variation of the resulting force with a change in the flow parameter. Here, an independent variable can be the Mach number, Reynolds number, or angle of attack. From the comparison graph of aerodynamic forces between the computation and the experiment, a user can confirm the accuracy of the CFD simulation and examine the tendency of the aerodynamic characteristics. However, sometimes the conducted simulation can fail to show the global tendency of aerodynamic characteristics. When this happens, the PSS (Parametric Study Service) can be used for additional computations with different flow parameters. In the PSS, a user selects the starting and ending ranges of the flow property. Then, the PSS automatically creates sub-cases with intermediate flow ranges, and requests HTC (high throughput computing) operations. The results of the aerodynamic characteristics can then be viewed again using e-AIRSplot, and the flow field data of each sub-case is accessible via e-DAVA.

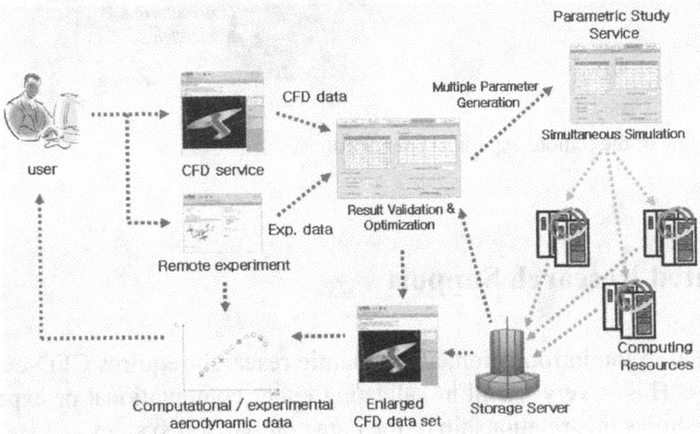

Fig. 6. Overview of integrated research: Parametric Study Service

7 Collaborative Conference System

Remote conferencing on e-AIRS is managed by the AGTk (Access Grid Toolkit), and the concept is shown in Fig. 7. When a user needs a remote discussion with other researchers, the user can create a new AG session, and see the session information on the e-AIRS portal. The host can also include participants from the user list on the portal, and the portal server will automatically send e-mail notices to the requested participants. Then, they can participate in the remote conference either by directly accessing the session or by following the link to the session, which is presented on the portal.

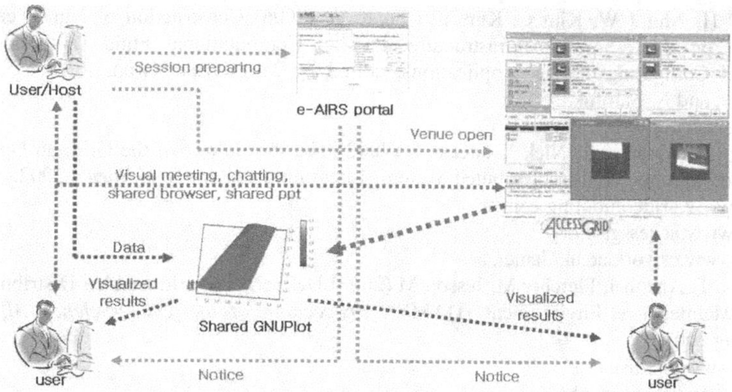

Fig. 7. Overview of the e-AIRS collaboration service

8 Conclusion

e-AIRS provides an easy-to-use integrated research/education environment for aerodynamic simulation and experiment. Through the portal interface, even non-experts can produce their own research outputs without having detailed knowledge of the Grid computing architecture. The portal with many service modules and user-friendly UI makes the research environment more convenient and collaborative. By e-AIRS, various computational and experimental services have been continually improved, and a reliable support can be given to computational and experimental researchers. Currently, the system focuses on being more generalized and performing more advanced services for integrated and collaborative research. With the success of those issues, e-AIRS is expected to be developed as a powerful aerodynamic research system, and it could be presented a good guideline for a future aerospace engineering research system using e-Science environment.

Acknowledgments The current work is a product of 'Development of e-Science technology for fluid dynamic research in various fields' project. The authors are grateful to Korea Institute of Science and Technology Information for their financial support.

References

[1] Kim Y, Kim E, Kim J Y, Cho J, Kim C, Cho K W (2006) e-AIRS: An e-Science Collaboration Portal for Aerospace Application. *HPCC 2006, LNCS(Lecture Note in Computer Science)* **4208**: 813-822.

[2] Kim J H, Ahn J W, Kim C, Kim Y, Cho K W (2006) Construction of Numerical Wind Tunnel on the e-Science Infrastructure. Parallel Computational Fluid Dynamics 2006: Parallel Computing and its Applications, edited by Jang-Hyuk Kwon, A. Ecer, Jacques Periaux, and N. Satofuka.
[3] http://e-science.or.kr/.
[4] Foster I, Kesselman C, Nick J, Tuecke S (2002) The Physiology of the Grid: an Open Grid Services Architecture for Distributed Systems Integration. *Global Grid Forum* 2002.
[5] http://www.gridcomputing.com/.
[6] http://www.accessgrid.org/.
[7] http://www.cs.york.ac.uk/dame/.
[8] Jackson T, Austin J, Fletcher M, Jessop M (2003) Delivering a Grid enabled Distributed Aircraft Maintenance Environment (DAME). *Proceeding of the UK e-Science All Hands Meeting* 2003.
[9] http://www.geodise.org/.
[10] http://www.wesc.ac.uk/.
[11] Crowther W J, Lunnon I, Wood N J, Davies A G, Hurst D, Coulton D G. A (2005) Grid Enabled Wind Tunnel Test System (GEWiTTS): Towards Real Time Integration of CFD and Experiment. *Proceeding of the 2nd Integrating CFD and Experiment in Aerodynamics international symposium* 2005. (http://www.cfd4aircraft.com/int_conf/IC2/proceedings/papers/w_crowther.pdf)
[12] http://www.dlr.de/sc/en/desktopdefault.aspx/tabid-1276/1760_read-3149.
[13] http://www.darwin.arc.nasa.gov/docs/.
[14] http://www.gridsphere.org/.
[15] http://www.dantecdynamics.com/piv/princip/index.html.

An Approach to Integrated Design, Analysis and Data Management for Rapid Air Vehicle Design

Ji Hong Kim*

Korea Aerospace Industries, Ltd., Korea – kimjh@koreaaero.com

Abstract An integrated system based on the fusion of proven legacy system and modern PIDO technology has been developed for aircraft configuration development in conceptual and preliminary design phase of aircraft development. KAI-RAVSIM proved successfully the feasibility of new integrated configuration development system by reducing design cycle time and enhancing the design capability. KAI-RAVSIM is currently expanding to be utilized with simulation data management system.

1 Introduction

The paradigm of aircraft development technology in 21st century is shifting from last century's 'Faster, Farther, Higher' to 'Quicker, Better, Cheaper' development. Korea Aerospace Industries, Ltd.(KAI) has established a full spectrum of aircraft development technologies for all phases and various types of aircrafts through full scale developments of basic trainer KT-1, advanced jet trainer and light attack aircraft T-50, UAV, and utility helicopter KHP programs. However, in order to remain an industry leader and to meet growing Korean domestic market requirements for new aircraft developments, emphasis must be placed on producing an optimum final product through an more efficient and leaner process than ever before.

The aircraft configuration development process is an inherently multi-disciplinary activity that requires different models and tools for various aspects of the design. The configuration which defined in the initial design phase has big impact on overall development program in terms of making a right and timely go-ahead decision with estimated performance, cost and schedule in the following phases.

In KAI, aircraft configuration development process in conceptual design phase is well established which constitute company knowledge base through a number of previous development programs as shown in Fig. 1. Although the development

O.-H. Byeon et al. (eds.), *Future Application and Middleware Technology on e-Science*,
DOI 10.1007/978-1-4419-1719-5_2, © Springer Science+Business Media, LLC 2010

process and tools are well proven through the real aircraft developments, but the system is legacy and needs a technical innovation for more rapid and faithful configuration developments. In recent conceptual design study for a new aircraft, although reliable engineering analyses data for each iterative configuration were obtained, but only a limited number of trade studies were conducted with the existing legacy system.

KAI-RAVSIM(Rapid Air Vehicle Simulation) development was planned to allow more rapid, efficient, reliable, and flexible configuration development capability in the growing number of advanced development programs.

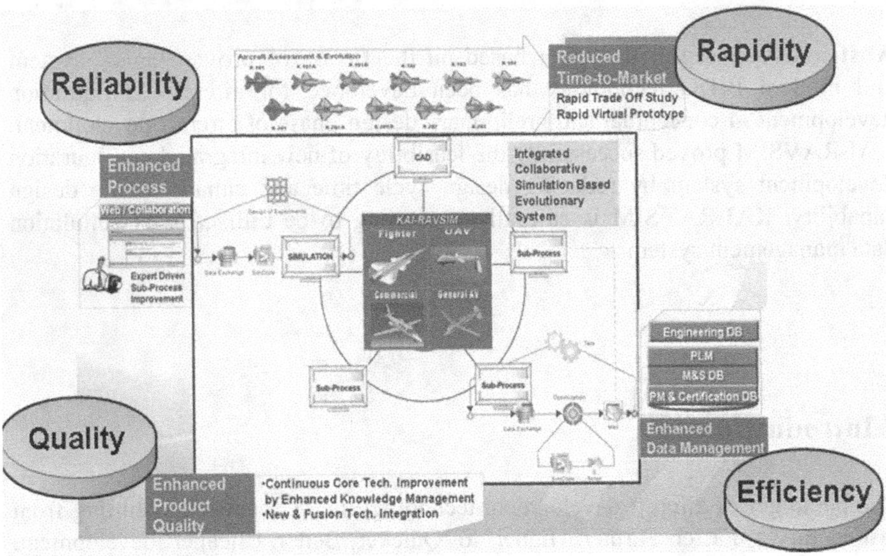

Fig. 1. Aircraft Conceptual Design Process

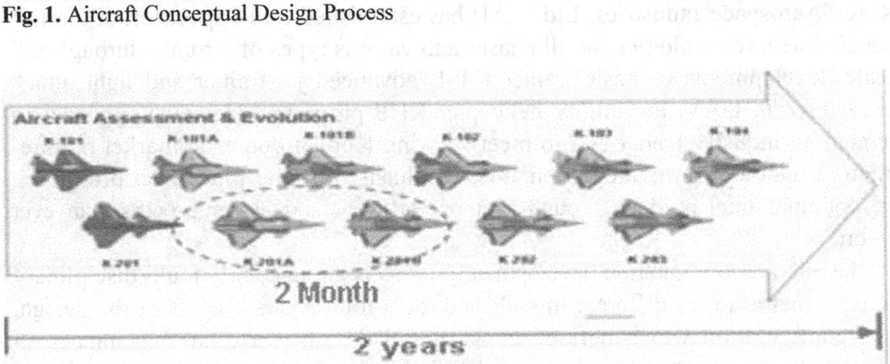

Fig. 2. Interactive Design Example

2 Development Concept

The key requirement of the new system is the integration of existing process with preserving the proven capability of legacy system. With modern commercial design tools for PIDO (Process Integration and Design Optimization) that permit greater integration of system components and functions, and with legacy and continually increasing computer power that allows these tools to be effectively integrated. Hence the main features of the new system should have the capability for process integration, automation, collaboration environment, knowledge based system, and expert driven evolutionary system in each discipline level as well as aircraft synthesis level.

In order to transform the existing legacy system successfully into a new integrated system, the modernization of core legacy softwares are also required. The core software modernization development such as in low fidelity aerodynamic analysis codes using panel and empirical methods, performance, stability and control, weight and balance, propulsion, cost analysis are proceeded separately with process integration projects.

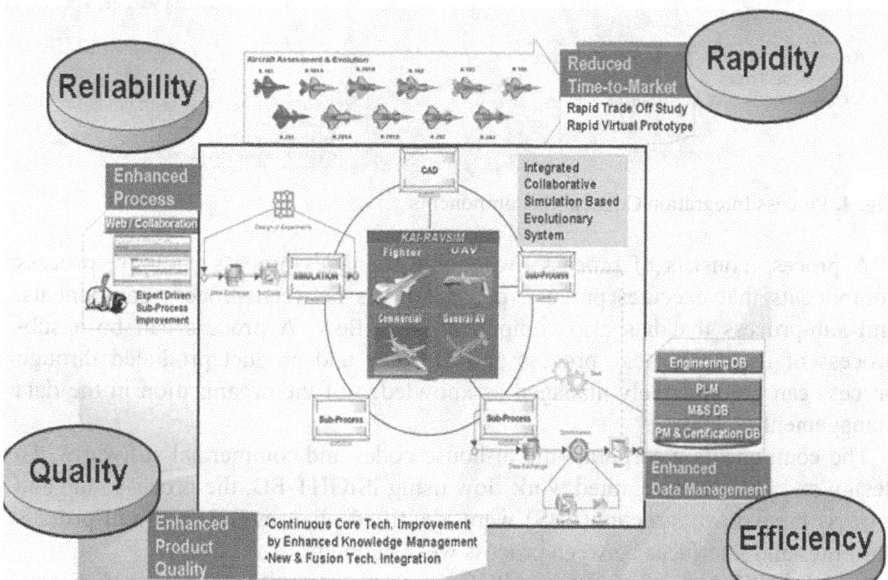

Fig. 3. KAI-RAVSIM Concept

The development of KAI-RAVSIM was performed incrementally. After the proof of concept project for validating the feasibility of process integration in a few discipline areas was performed, the level of integration was expanded gradually.

3 Process Integration and Design Optimization

A process can be defined a series of operations, procedures or activities for an object product.

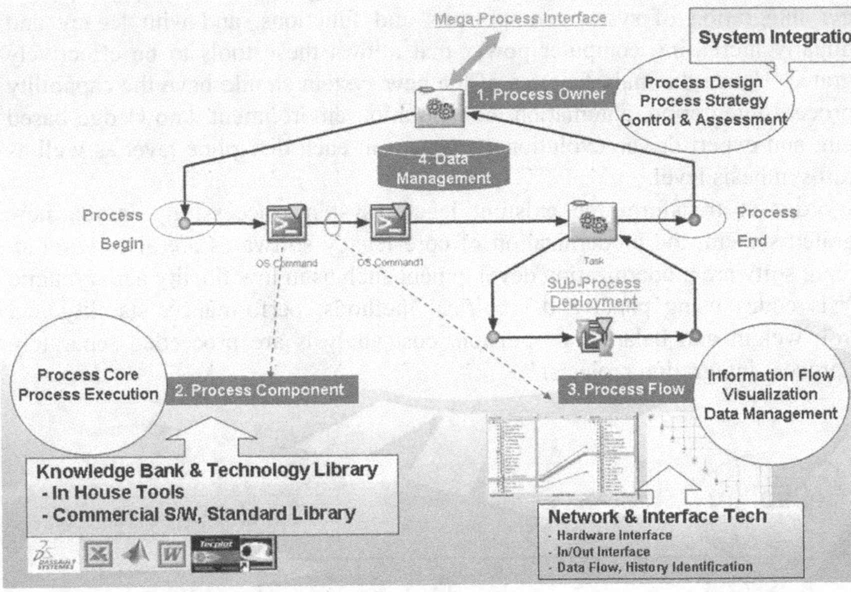

Fig. 4. Process Integration Concept & Components

A process consists of process owner that manages process strategy, process components that executes process, process flows between process components, and sub-process that has also components and flow. A process can be a sub-process of its upper mega process and the data and product produced through process can be effectively managed as knowledge of the organization in the data management system.

The components incorporate the in-house codes and commercial softwares. To design and build an integrated work flow using iSIGHT-FD, the process map and process breakdown structure(PBS) were identified over level 5 or 6 and process attributes and interfaces between process were defined.

KAI-RAVSIM proof of concept(POC) project were proceeded according to 6 sigma's DFSS(Design for Six Sigma) roadmap. The system requirements and development strategy are thoroughly defined through critical customer requirement (CCR) review in the early development phase.

The process integration of five disciplines at first and currently of eight disciplines have completed including aero-analysis, stability & control, weight & balance, propulsion, performance, sizing, cost and configuration. The integration of each discipline's process was proceeded by each expert group using iSIGHT-FD and expanded to aircraft synthesis process in Fiper environment.

Fig. 5. KAI-RAVSIM

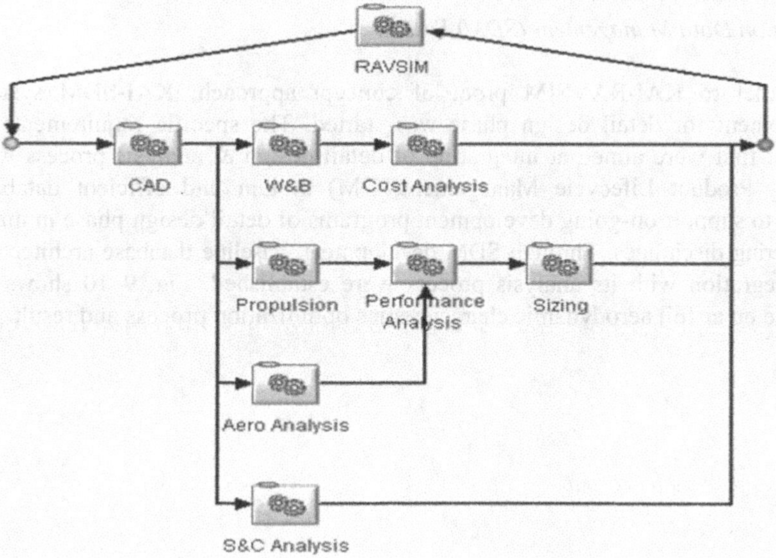

Fig. 6. Integrated Work Flow of KAI-RAVSIM

One of the CTQs(Critical To Quality) to measure the success of POC projects was the level of integration and lead-time reduction. Fig. 7 shows that the initial achievement in lead time reduction in POC phase is nearly half of the before-process.

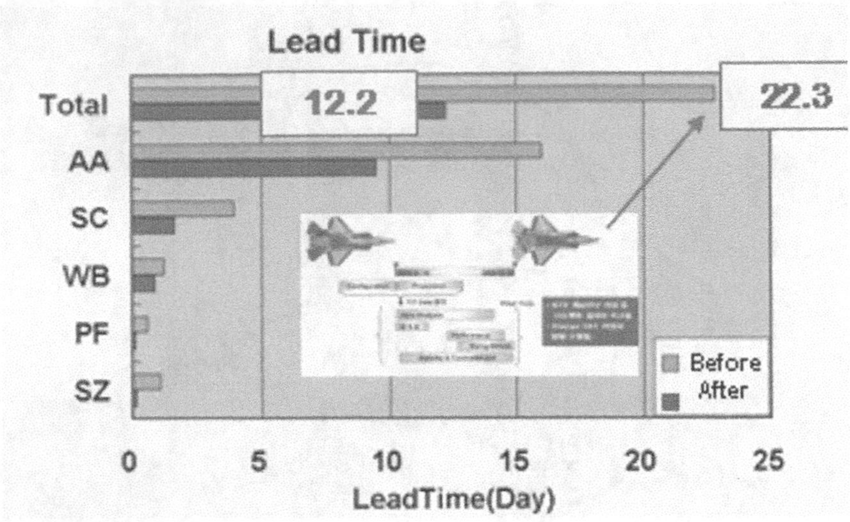

Fig. 7. Lead Time Reduction in KAI-RAVSIM POC Phase

Simulation Data Management (SDM) System

In parallel to KAI-RAVSIM proof of concept approach, KAI-SDM system development for detail design phase was started. The specific requirements of SDM at first were aimed at integration of detail design & analysis process with existing Product Lifecycle Management(PLM) system and efficient database system to support on-going development programs of detail design phase in many engineering disciplines. Through SDM development, baseline database architecture and integration with its analysis process were established. Fig. 9–10 shows an example on airfoil aerodynamic characteristics optimization process and result.

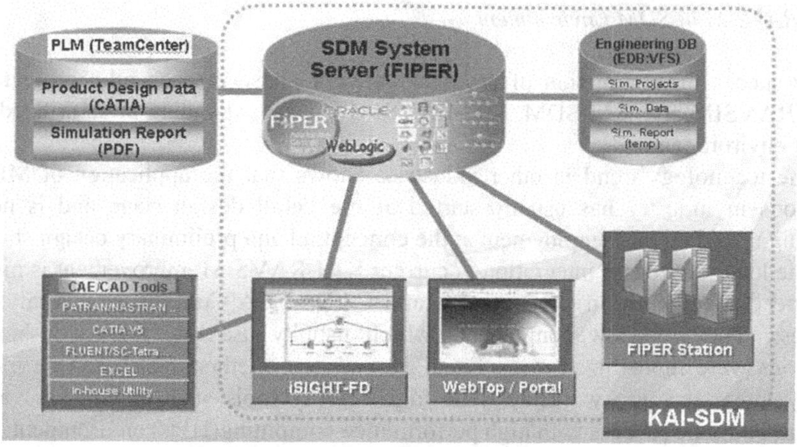

Fig. 8. Simulation Data Management System

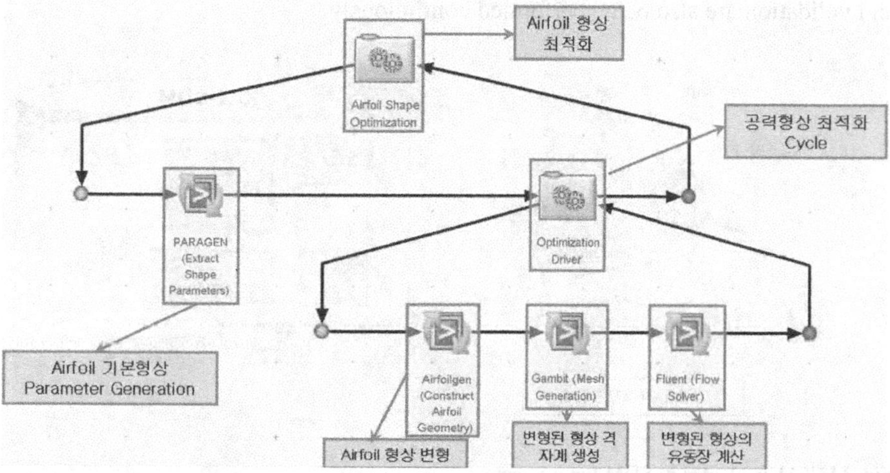

Fig. 9. Optimization Process

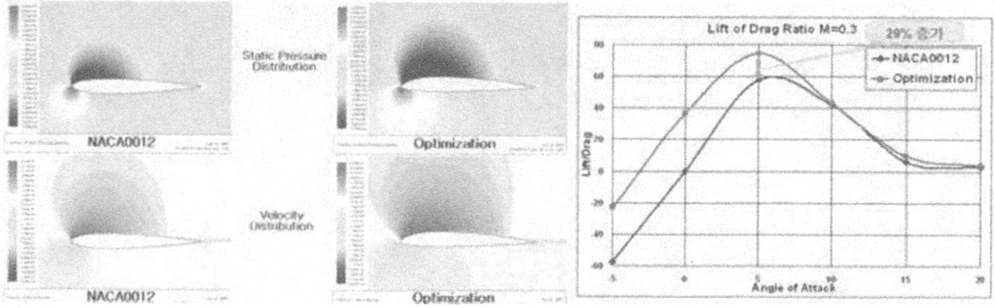

Fig. 10. Optimization Results

KAI-RAVSIM in SDM Environment

After successful completion of proof of concept phase in each pilot project of KAI-RAVSIM and KAI-SDM, KAI-RAVSIM is now expanding to be utilized in SDM environment.

The technology trend in other industries shows that the application of MDO methods in industry has usually started at the detail design stage and is now moving upstream into employment at the conceptual and preliminary design stage.

The level of process integration in current KAI-RAVSIM improvement is more enhanced specifically in CAD process and CAD to CA(Configuration Analysis) process. The workflow components which usually use low fidelity in-house methods were modernized using Excel Spreadsheet method which can be more easily integrated into workflow. The high fidelity tools such as CFD are also integrated in the process with high performance computing(HPC) environment.

In addition to process integration and automation, to achieve ultimate goal for MDO in aircraft synthesis level, an effort for process reconstruction, improvement and validation are also being performed continuously.

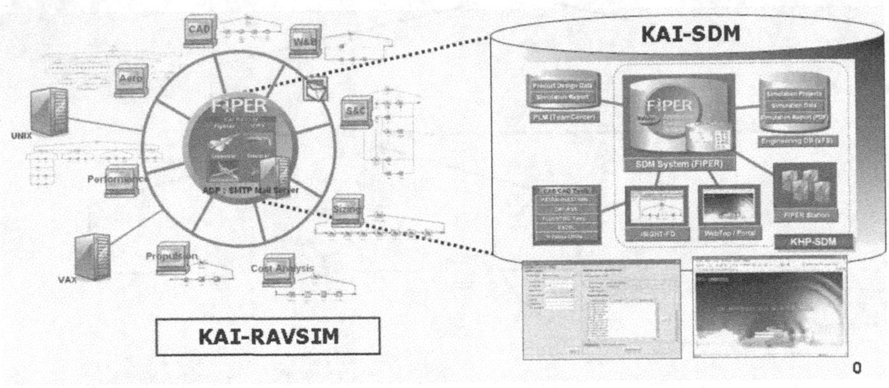

Fig. 11. KAI-RAVSIM in SDM Environment

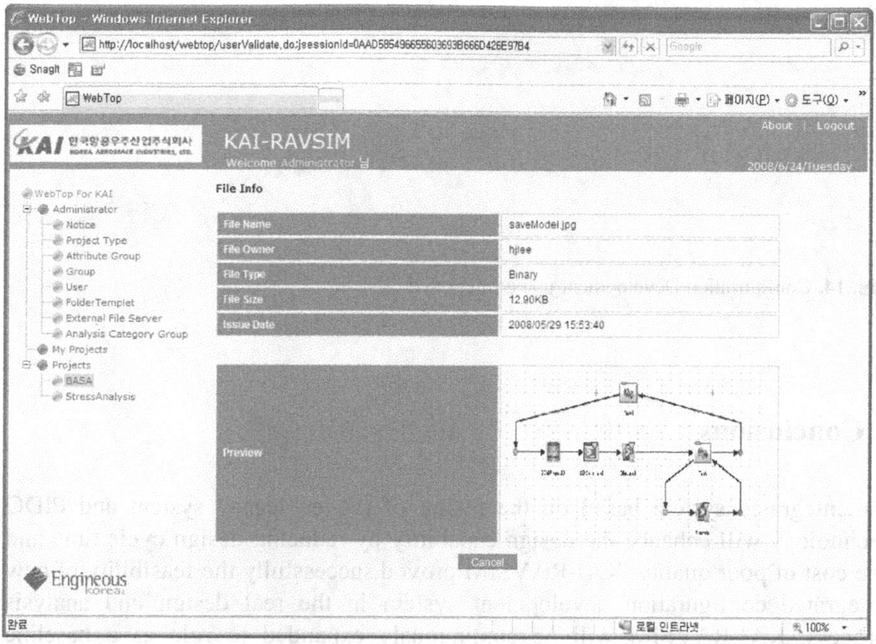

Fig. 12. KAI-RAVSIM Webtop System

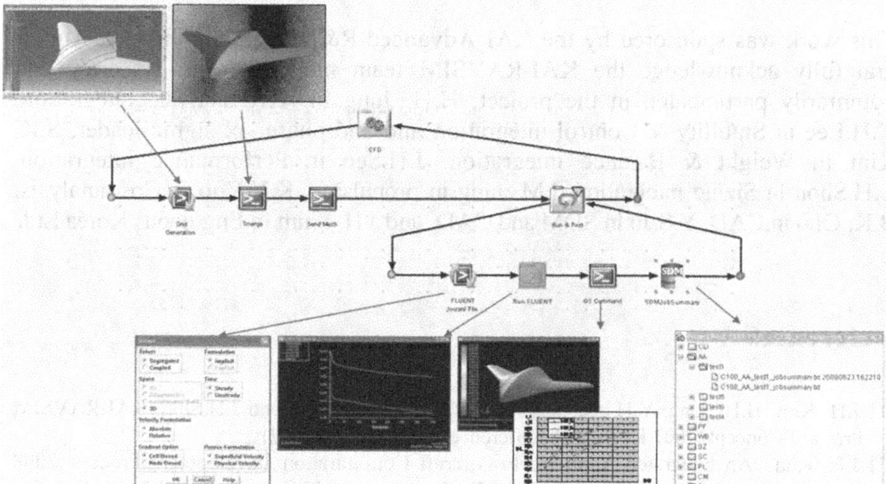

Fig. 13. Integrated CFD Workflow

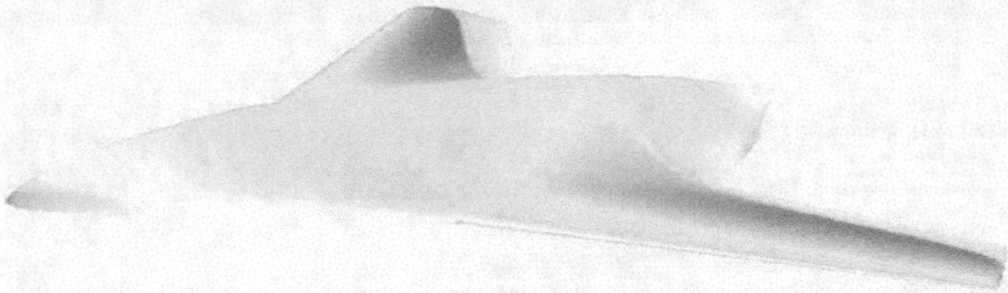

Fig. 14. Configuration Development using Integrated System

4 Conclusions

An integrated system based on the fusion of proven legacy system and PIDO technology will enhance the design capability by reducing design cycle time and the cost of poor quality. KAI-RAVSIM proved successfully the feasibility of new integrated configuration development system in the real design and analysis process. KAI-RAVSIM will be continuously expanded to role as a baseline development system in the new aircraft development program.

Acknowledgements

This work was sponsored by the KAI Advanced R&D Programs budget. Author gratefully acknowledge the KAI-RAVSIM team members who sincerely and voluntarily participated in the project; H.H. Jung in Aero-analysis integration, Y.H.Lee in Stability & Control integration and 2nd phase six sigma leader, S.K. Kim in Weight & Balance integration, J.H.Seo in Performance integration, C.H.Shon in Sizing integration, I.M. Jung in propulsion, K.Y.Yoo in Cost analysis, B.K. Oho in CAD, Y.S.Ju in SDM and CAD, and J.H. Shim in Engineous Korea Ltd.

References

[1] J.H. Kim, H.H. Jung, Y.H.Lee, S.K.Kim, C.H.Shon, J.H.Seo. and J.H.Shim:KAI-RAVSIM Proof of Concept, 2007 KSAS fall conference, Jeju, Korea, (2007)
[2] J.H. Kim, :An Integrated Approach to Aircraft Configuration Development Process, 2008 European Symposium and Seminar Series, Engineous, Munich, Germany, April 14-15, (2008).
[3] O. Weck, J. Agte., J. S. Sobieski, P. Arendsen, A. Morris, and M. Spieck, "Sate-of-the-Art and Future Trends in Multidisciplinary Design Optimization", AIAA 2007-1905
[4] K.G. Bowcutt, "A Perspective on the Future of Aerospace Vehicle Design", AIAA 2003-69

Development of v-DMU Based on e-Science Using COVISE and SAGE

Suchul Shin[*], Yuna Kang[*], Hyokwang Lee[*], Byungchul Kim[†], Soonhung Han[‡], Jongbae Moon[◊], Kum Won Cho[◊]

Korea Advanced Institute of Science and Technology[*‡], PartDB Co., Ltd., Korea[†] Institute of Science and Technology Information[◊]
{eva317, balbal86, adpc9}@icad.kaist.ac.kr[*], mir7942@partdb.com[†], shhan@kaist.ac.kr[‡], {jbmoon, ckw}@kisti.re.kr[◊]

Abstract Virtual digital mock-up (v-DMU) refers to all of the activities in the design, analysis, and visualization of the product in a 3D virtual environment that lead to a lower cost and a higher quality. In the early days, designers exchanged CAD files directly in collaborations. Recently, DMU systems have been used for relatively effective designs that generally support distributed and collaborative design capability by sharing the design data via the Internet. However, a range of problems can arise in such a case. In the case of large-scale products such as aircrafts or ships, the data size can be on a scale so large that it requires large amount of space on the workstation and requires considerable time for exchanges. Moreover, security problems often occur in the process of data exchanges. For a company and a nation, this can be crucial. The immersive visualization of product design data is becoming more important in collaborative design. As a solution to these issues, this paper proposes a new approach using the technology of the remote visualization of CAD data. This involves the streaming of rendered graphics using COVISE and SAGE. This paper also introduces the implementation of v-DMU based on e-Science by remote visualization.

1. Introduction

The need for collaborative product design in global companies is increasing due to globalization, the rapid product development cycle, and the rapid development of information technology. In addition, the key features of collaborative CAD are moving to human-to-human interaction from human-to-computer interaction [1]. To meet this demand, several large-scale studies have been done, and countless technologies have been developed. Nevertheless, many problems remain unsolved. One of these problems involves the need for collaborative visualization.

O.-H. Byeon et al. (eds.), *Future Application and Middleware Technology on e-Science*,
DOI 10.1007/978-1-4419-1719-5_3, © Springer Science+Business Media, LLC 2010

Several conventional approaches have been used for the visualization of product design data (normally CAD data) in a collaborative design environment. The easiest means of realizing this involves exchanging physical files including CAD models. If designers work on the same design system, they can view the data by exchanging data files or sharing a repository. If design systems are different so that one designer cannot view data created by an original system directly, translation of the data into a format that can be read on the second system becomes necessary. However, translation technology among commercial CAD systems has not yet been perfected, implying that a loss of design information can occurs in the process of translation. This can leave users unable to visualize the data correctly in the event of breakage or a loss of geometry information. Additionally, with very large data sets, a user who wants to view the data should wait until it downloads completely, which exceeds practical limits for working concurrently. Therefore, a more effective approach is required.

Security in collaborative product design is another important issue because the vital technologies of a company could be intercepted in the process of exchanging design data. If CAD files are exchanged directly, it is possible to receive all of the product design information. Using VRML, X3D and 3D streaming (Sec. 2), only mesh information is received, omitting the information of the assembly and design features. However, there would be no company that wants even a portion of the product data to be stolen.

Another issue of product design is the immersive visualization of a virtual prototype. Visualization on a monitor is sufficient for small-scale products such as an engine, but it is difficult to evaluate very large products such as automobiles, ships and aircraft in this manner. Hence, large-scale visualization is necessary, and this requires special tools and high-end workstations. According to the proposed approach, even a user with a basic personal computer can experience an immersive visualization in its actual size without a design data file.

In order to achieve this, the technology of streaming frames of rendered images of 3D objects is proposed in this paper.

2. Related Work

Recently, web-based visualization has become widely used for collaboration because the Internet has encircled the globe. Many web-based visualization systems have been developed to support the visualization, annotation and inspection of design models to provide assistance with distributed design and manufacturing activities [2]. The Web is one of the most popularly used Internet tools as it provides a light-weight and an operation-system-independent platform for users to search, browse, retrieve and manipulate information disseminated and shared remotely. In order to visualize 3D objects effectively on the Web, several concise formats, such as VRML, X3D, W3D and MPEG-4, have been launched [3].

However, it is not easy to share updated data in real time because it takes a very long time to download large CAD files for systems such as airplanes, ships and automobiles. Therefore, a new scheme for visualization was presented by Gueziec [4] and Fuh [3] involving 3D streaming technology, which is similar to the conventional streaming of video and audio. As streaming is utilized, users do not need to download the entire CAD file before visualization. They can see a portion of the data even before downloading is completed. However, in contrast to video-streaming, this method does not transmit the meshes for CAD models as continuous streams; instead, it generates a simplified model and refines it to the original. However, this is closer to a progressive approach such as GIF as opposed to streaming. Fig. 1 [5] shows the 3D streaming technology, and Table 1 lists the commercial collaborative visualization tools and classifies their visualization approaches.

Another approach is to exchange the internal data structure of the memory, generally RAM, which is usually faster and smaller than a physical file. Collaborative Visualization and Simulation Environment (COVISE) is one such technology taking this approach. It has architecture that supports exchanges of internal data. It is a scientific visualization tool developed at HLRS, the high-performance computing center in Stuttgart, Germany. COVISE on each workstation has its own shared data space, and users exchange shared data through the COVISE Request Broker (CRB) [6]. However, this approach is weak in terms of security, as internal data can be accessed in some cases.

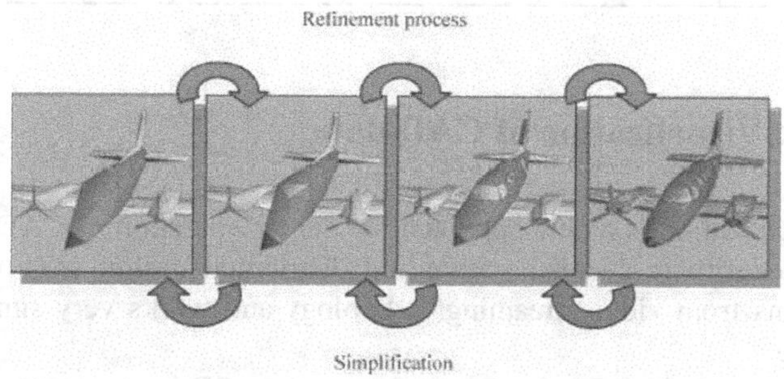

Fig. 1. Visual effects of the mesh simplification and refinement processes [5]

As technologies to stream 3D information, the Scalable Adaptive Graphics Environment (SAGE) [7], WireGL [8], Chromium [9] and Aura [10] generally use the method streaming rendered frames or manipulating streams of graphics API commands. Their goal is visualization on a scalable tiled display. This is suitable to the goals of the present study, as visualization computers do not require the original data, which implies that file downloading is unnecessary. Hence, security is enhanced.

Table 1. Visualization-based CAD systems [5]

Products	Characteristics and functions	Data distributed methods
Cimmetry Systems Autovue™	A viewer for part and assembly models View, mark-up, measure, explode, cross-section, etc	3D streaming
InFlow ConceptWorks™	An add-on viewer to SolidWorks View and mark-up	3D streaming
Actify SpinFire™	A viewer for part models View, cross-section, measure, grid and ru	Download
SolidWorks eDrawing™	A viewer for native or simplified SolidWorks files View, mark-up, measure, 3D pointer, animation	Download
Adaptive media envision 3D™	A viewer for part models View, mark-up, redline, chat	3D streaming
Centric Software Pivotal Studio™	A base platform to provide a workspace manager, a project organizer and a viewer for part models View, mark-up, video/audio conferencing, chat	Download/3D streaming
Hoops Streaming Toolkit™	A toolkit to provide 3D streaming APIs BaseStream class library, advanced compression, attribute (color, texture) support, object prioritization, etc	3D streaming
RealityWave ConceptStation™	A VizStream platform, which consists a server and a client View, mark-up, message	3D streaming
Autodesk Streamline™	A platform based on the VizStream View, measure, bill of materials	3D streaming

3. Remote Visualization of CAD data

Remote visualization is a new approach for the visualization of CAD data in real time with security in a collaborative and distributed design environment. This concept stems from video streaming technology and works very similarly to TV broadcasting.

Generally, video is defined as a set of continuous 2D images arranged in a time sequence. By streaming sequential frames, a video streamed over the Internet can be watched immediately without being in possession of the entire file. Each frame consists of pixels in size of the resolution of the video, which essentially requires a very large bandwidth because the frame rate for video is usually 15–30 fps. As a result, the frames are typically compressed using a standard codec.

The new approach suggested in this paper applies 2D the streaming technology to 3D visualization. 3D objects such as CAD models are rendered through a rendering pipeline by a graphics card. 2D images (frames) rendered in real time are printed on a monitor, and the experience is much like 3D video movement. The pixel values of each frame rendered can be accessed using a low-level graphical command, for example, glReadPixels(). By compressing the pixels and streaming them, designers at a remote site can view CAD data without downloading the CAD file.

There are three main advantages of the proposed method.

- It reduces the time to download: although the data may be very large, even as much as several gigabytes, the time needed to visualize it remotely equals that of a very small amount of data, for example, of a few kilobytes.
- Secure collaboration: only 2D images are exchanged; thus, information cannot be gleaned by others remotely.
- Large-scale visualization: the proposed method enables the visualization of a data-intensive product such as a ship or an automobile in the actual size on a large-scale tiled display.

4. Implementation

In order to stream out 3D scenes, SAGE and COVISE are used as a streaming tool and a post-processing and rendering tool, respectively. Sec 4.1 explains the reasoning behind the selection of COVISE and SAGE as implementation tools, and Sec 4.2 and Sec 4.3 describe the implementation of the remote visualization of CAD (CATIA V5) by integrating SAGE into COVISE. The cyber-infrastructure required for this system is then outlined in Sec 4.4.

4.1 COVISE / SAGE

The academic program COVISE was used for visualization of CAD data in this research, as it requires no licensing fees and because the rendering module of COVISE is open source software. It also provides various functionalities for scientific visualization as well as CAD data. Another strong point is its cross-platform design [6].

SAGE is a graphic streaming architecture supporting scientific visualization. This tool was used to stream the output of COVISE. Chromium also has a similar capability, but it is not designed to execute multiple applications on a tiled display, and its applications have a static layout on a tiled display [7].

4.2 Loading CAD files into COVISE

The commercial version of COVISE launched by VISENSO provides a CAD extension module which is available with interfaces for most CAD data formats [11]. However, the academic version of COVISE does not provide such a module. Hence, a new module able to import CAD data formats should be developed. In this research, several candidate methods were found for the loading of the CAD data format, particularly the CATIA v5 format. Fig. 2 shows these approaches with the loss of information data for each.

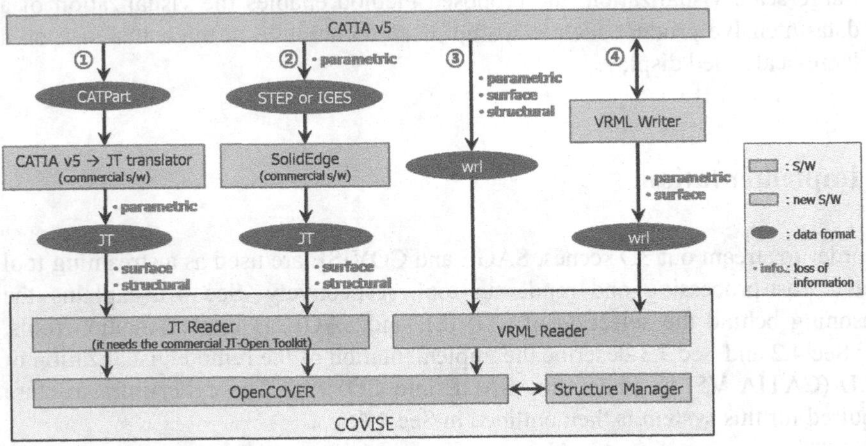

Fig. 2. 4 Four candidate approaches able to load CAD data into COVISE

JT is a mature lightweight data format that already enjoys widespread use in the automobile and aerospace industries and is equally suitable for all manufacturing industry applications. It holds associations to the original CAD information, assemblies, product structure, geometry, attributes, meta data and PMI [12]. HLRS has developed a JT reader module, but it does not hold such information apart from its tessellated geometry. Additionally, translators to convert CATIA v5 data into the JT format require a license fee as well as JT-Open Toolkit, which is needed to execute the JT reader.

Therefore, this study uses the VRML format because COVISE comes with a VRML reader and the quality is not worse than JT. In order to hold the structural information of CAD data, a VR writer was created by adding the structural information to the corresponding VRML file. This is handled by the plug-in module of COVISE, the structure manager.

4.3 Integration of SAGE and COVISE

CAD data could then be visualized by COVISE; thus, the result could be streamed out. SAGE provides the SAGE Application Interface Library (SAIL), which enables an application to stream its output. Most visualization applications can be integrated easily into the SAGE framework by adding a few lines of API code for SAIL [7].

COVISE has various rendering modules, including QtRenderer, VRRenderer and OpenCOVER. Among these modules, OpenCOVER is most powerful as it is based on OpenSceneGraph [13], an open source high-performance 3D graphics toolkit. Moreover, a plug-in customized by a user can be added. The plug-in for OpenCOVER is loaded dynamically at run time and runs coupled with OpenCOVER.

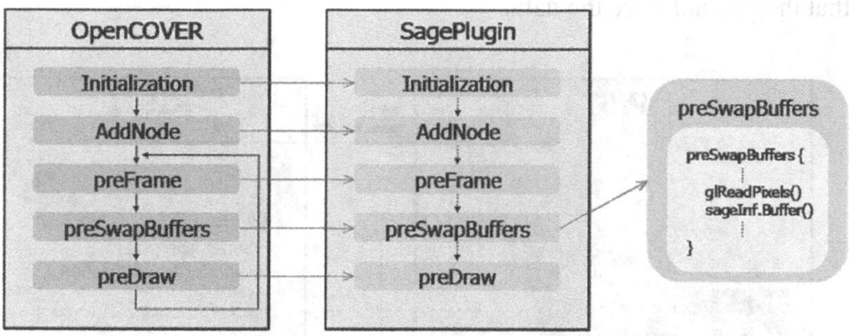

Fig. 3. SagePlugin's command flow

A new plug-in termed SagePlugin was developed. The preSwapBuffers() function of SagePlugin is called whenever the preSwapBuffers() functions of OpenCOVER is called. preSwapBuffers() contains two commands: glReadPixels() and sageInf.Buffer(). The current pixel array received by glReadPixels() is sent to SAGE by sageInf.Buffer(). It is then compressed and streamed. The relevant diagram of this is shown in Fig. 3.

4.4 High throughput networking

This system requires an ultra-high-bandwidth network because of the large size of the streamed packets. The iCAVE room at KAIST, an immersive virtual reality environment, was connected to KREONet2, Korea's national science & research network [14]. It provides 1-10Gbps access bandwidth and is linked abroad via GLORIAD linking scientists in the US, Russia, China, Korea, Canada, the

Netherlands and the Nordic countries via an advanced cyber-infrastructure [15]. A test is planned with KISTI, UCSD, Osaka Univ. and NCHC.

5. Experiment

Fig. 4 shows the scenario of this experiment. Three organizations participated in this experiment: WST, KISTI and KAIST. WST (Wing Ship Technology) is a R&D company of Wing-In-Ground (WIG), and KISTI is the super-computing center in Korea. WST designs a WIG with CATIA v5, and KISTI then analyzes the mesh data generated from GridGen. The COVISE tool receives and visualizes the design data and the analyzed data, and the result of the visualization is then streamed to WST, KAIST and KISTI. The designers at KAIST and KISTI can observe and check the design on a large-scale tiled display in real time, despite the fact that they do not have the data.

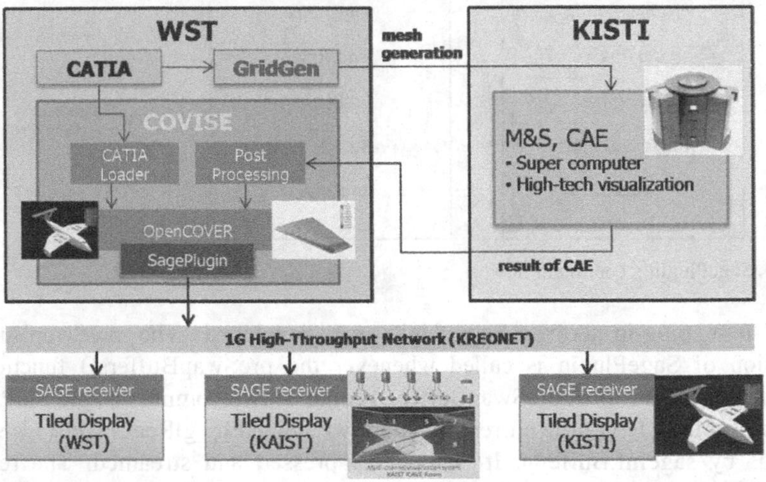

Fig. 4. Scenario of the experiment for the remote visualization of CAD/CAE data

6. Conclusion / Future Work

This paper proposes a new approach to visualize CAD/CAE data at remote sites in a collaborative and distributed product design environment. The steps of this approach are given below.

- Step 1: Render CAD/CAE data
- Step 2: Obtain pixels of the rendered image at each frame
- Step 3: Compress the pixels using a standard codec
- Step 4: Stream the compressed pixels in real time
- Step 5: Receive them and visualize then on a tiled display

Using this approach, it is possible to view and check the CAD/CAE data at remote sites without downloading the data files. This implies that only the owner can obtain the data, although users can observe it. Therefore, the proposed method greatly increases the level of security in collaborative product designs. It also supports the functionality to visualize on a tiled display so that large-scale products such as automobiles can be visualized in their actual sizes easily.

The proposed method was implemented by integrating SAGE into the plug-in of OpenCOVER in COVISE with SAIL. In order to load CAD data into COVISE, the data was converted into the VRML format.

However, the translated data in the VRML format was not identical to the original data. Hence, technology to read CAD data directly or to integrate SAGE into commercial CAD systems should be researched. Another problem is the requirement of ultra-high bandwidth networks, which are not yet popular and are currently expensive. Although these networks will likely become popular in the future, research into ways to reduce the minimum bandwidth required for this system is essential.

Acknowledgments This research was supported by the project "Development of the v-DMU based on COVISE", which was funded by the Korea Institute of Science and Technology Information.

References

[1] He F, Han S (2006) A method and tool for human-human interaction and instant collaboration in CSCW-based CAD. Computers in Industry. 57(8-9):740-751

[2] Li WD (2005) A Web-based service for distributed process planning optimization. Computers in Industry. 56(3):272-288

[3] Fuh JYH, Li WD (2004) Advances in collaborative CAD: the-state-of-the art. Computer-Aided Design. 37(5):571-581

[4] Gueziec A, Taubin G, Horn B et al (1999) A framework for streaming geometry in VRML. IEEE Computer Graphics and Applications. 19(2):68-78

[5] Li WD, Lu WF, Fuh JYH et al (2005) Collaborative computer-aided design--research and development status. Computer-Aided Design. 37(9):931-940

[6] COVISE. http://www.hlrs.de/organization/vis/covise. Accessed 12 May 2008

[7] Renambot L, Jeong B, Jagodic R et al (2006) Collaborative Visualization using High-Resolution Tiled Displays. ACM CHI Workshop on Inf Visualization Interact

[8] Humphreys G, Buck I, Eldridge M et al (2000) Distributed rendering for scalable displays. IEEE Supercomputing 2000

[9] Humphreys G, Houston M, Ng Y et al (2002) Chromium: A stream-processing framework for interactive rendering on clusters. Proc of SIGGRAPH 2002.
[10] Germans D, Spoelder HJW, Renambot L et al (2001) VIRPI: A high-level toolkit for interactive scientific visualization in virtual reality. Proc IPT/Eurographics VE Workshop.
[11] VISENSO. http://www.visenso.de. Accessed 06 September 2008
[12] JT Open. http://www.jtopen.com. Accessed 23 August 2008
[13] OpenSceneGraph. http://www.openscenegraph.org. Accessed 02 June 2008
[14] KREONET. http://www.kreonet.re.kr. Accessed 07 July 2008
[15] GLORIAD. http://www.gloriad.org. Accessed 15 June 2008

Design of a Four Degree_of_Freedom Manipulator for Northern Light Mars Mission

Regina Lee (a), Brendan Quine (b), Kartheephan Sathiyanathan (c), Caroline Roberts (d) and the Northern Light team

Assistant Professor, Department Earth and Space Science and Engineering, PSE134 York University, 4700 Keele Street, Toronto, Ontario M3J 1P3 (416) 736-2100 ext 22095, reginal@yorku.ca

Assistant Professor, Department Earth and Space Science and Engineering, PSE256 York University, 4700 Keele Street, Toronto, Ontario M3J 1P3, also Technical Director, Thoth Technology Inc., 16845 Jane St RR1 Kettleby, ON L0G 1J0 Canada, also, (905) 713-2884, ben@thoth.ca

Masters' of Science Candidates, Department Earth and Space Science and Engineering, PSE002B York University, 4700 Keele Street, Toronto, Ontario M3J 1P3 (416) 736-2100 ext 33589, kingk@yorku.ca

President and Chief Executive Officer, Thoth Technology Inc., 16845 Jane St RR1 Kettleby, ON L0G 1J0 Canada, also, (905) 713-2884, caroline@thoth.ca

Abstract Northern Light is a Canadian mission to Mars, currently developed by a team of engineers, scientists and industrial organizations. The mission objectives include scientific goals such as the search for life and water, preparation for a sample return and engineering goals including the demonstration of interplanetary travel, an entry, descent and landing system, a rover design, a manipulator/drilling system, and semi-autonomous control in remote operations. The Northern Light team at York University is developing a four degree-of-freedom manipulator system, specifically for this remote operation. The Northern Light manipulator system will be mounted directly on the lander (not on the rover), providing an opportunity to perform scientific missions directly from the lander. The drilling instrument, to be mounted on the manipulator, is currently under development by Dr. Tze Chuen Ng now with the help of Hong Kong's Polytechnics University. The operation concept is based on a "single command cycle" approach. The operation plans are designed to handle exceptions, failures and unforeseen events using local intelligence and a contingency planner.

O.-H. Byeon et al. (eds.), *Future Application and Middleware Technology on e-Science*, DOI 10.1007/978-1-4419-1719-5_4, © Springer Science+Business Media, LLC 2010

1 Introduction

Northern Light is a robotic Mars lander system equipped with sophisticated scientific instruments to examine the Martian surface and atmosphere. The proposed lander design features a complete entry, descent, and landing system that can support a number of scientific experiments and advanced engineering technologies. Thoth Technology is leading the commercial development while York University is leading the scientific and engineering research aspect of the mission. The Northern Light mission objective is to place one or more landers on the surface of Mars to perform scientific analysis while performing engineering technology demonstrations. The Northern Light team consists of over 50 scientists and researchers in Canada and around the world.

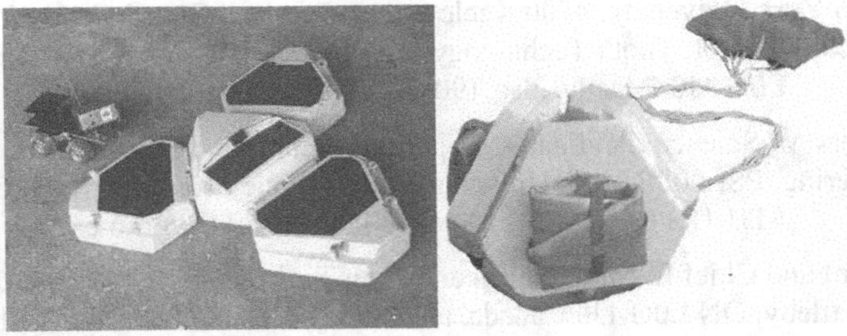

Fig. 1. Northern Light, Thoth Technology

In section 0 of this paper, the mission objectives and overall architecture is briefly described. In sections 0 through 0, the Northern Light manipulator system is described in detail. The research team at York University has examined the mass and volume constraints that the lander imposes on the manipulator and proposed a simple four degrees-of-freedom (DOF) direct-drive system. The functional prototype has been manufactured in the laboratory and the kinematic modeling and analysis are well under way. In section 0, the support facility for the Northern Light mission, including the 46-meter radio observatory is briefly discussed.

This Canadian Mars mission will provide extensive new information on the Martian atmosphere, surface and subsurface. The mission will also enable Canadian institutes and international partners to develop advanced technology and engineering designs for interplanetary exploration and remote operations. This paper provides an overview of the mission with the focus on the drilling operation.

2 Northern Lights Mission Overview

The Northern Light mission was designed with five distinctive objectives in mind: search for life, search for water, investigate the atmosphere and radiation balance, prepare for a sample-return mission, and perform life-science experiments. Unlike similar Mars missions in the past, the Northern Light mission aims to deploy an instrumentation package directly from the lander as well as the rover, providing the redundancy. This redundant design of the apparatus provides economy and ensures that primary science objectives can be met without rover deployment.

Using the series of instruments discussed in section 0, several scientific experiments are planned. The Martian atmosphere will be examined to look for biomarker gases and compositional variations, and to prepare for future human exploration. Also, a spectroscopic examination of the surface and the immediate subsurface will be conducted to look for signs of life, water and radiation flux. Three-dimensional subsurface imaging using ground-penetrating radar is also planned for further search for water and life.

The Northern Light system is comprised of several subsystems: entry, descent, and landing (EDL) system, lander avionics and structure, and lander instrumentation including a manipulator arm. A deployable rover is also under consideration. The EDL system (shown in Fig. 1) is to transfer the lander safely from the delivery spacecraft to the surface of Mars. The Northern Light lander is made of an advanced composite material that includes thermal shielding and shock absorption. The compact design was originally based on the Beagle 2 Lander developed by EADS Astrium Ltd. Based on the lessons learned from the Beagle 2 mission, the Northern Light lander was modified to feature more robust structure and compact design with minimum moving parts and automatic deployment mechanisms. The lander is equipped with a manipulator arm (not shown in Fig. 1) to perform scientific experiments from the landing site. Refer to [1] for more information on the Northern Light system.

The Northern Light mission operations will be managed by a team of scientists and engineers with Thoth technology as the managing institute. A team of highly skilled technicians will track the host spacecraft from the launch site to the landing site on Mars from the Algonquin Radio Observatory (ARO). The science team at York University has been working closely with instruments similar to the Northern Light instruments. The data down-linked and transferred from ARO will be stored and distributed from the operations center. The normal and contingency operations procedure will be reviewed and implemented from this location.

3. Northern Light Manipulator System

The Northern Light lander is equipped with a four degree-of-freedom (DOF) manipulator. Fig. 2 shows the manipulator carrying four instruments: a high-definition camera, a panoramic camera, the Argus spectrometer and the TC Corer.

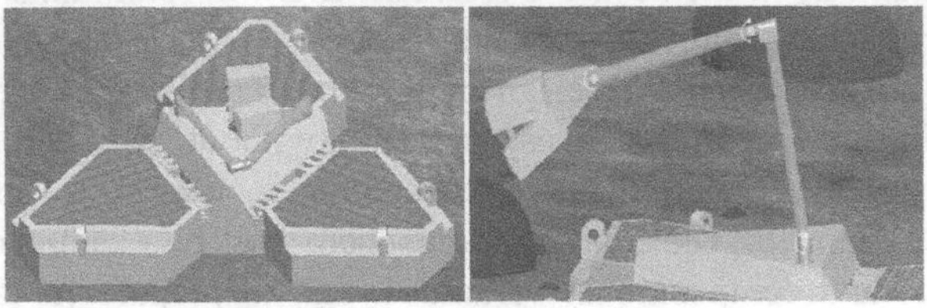

Fig. 2. Stowed and deployed arm configuration

3.1 Requirements and Constraints

The Northern Light lander places stringent constraints on the manipulator design due to the limited volume within the landing vehicle and the limited mass allowed for the arm with the instruments at the distal end. The total mass of the lander instruments that will be attached to the manipulator is 1.0 kg. Moreover, the arm itself cannot weigh more than 1.5 kg. The instruments need to be lifted at a length of 60 cm. The requirements for low-mass and compact storage implied a simple design with the minimum degrees of freedom to achieve the drilling task. Reduction in degrees of freedom yields a reduction in joint mechanisms, which in turn implies reduced mass, power and complexity.

An additional requirement was imposed on the design to sustain the weight of the instruments and itself under Earth's gravitational field (1-g), so that the functional tests can be carried out without additional test instrumentation. In [2], the authors argue that space robotic systems need to be tested only by simulations or hardware-in-the-loop emulation since they "cannot operate in 1-g environment". In order to avoid such complicated and expensive experimental setup, the Northern Light manipulator was designed to operate in a 1-g environment. The system is expected to survive in a harsh Mars environment for several months, while collecting science data and taking images.

The design was also constrained by the cost factors. While no budgetary restriction has been imposed on the manipulator development, the team focused on the most cost-effective, simple to assemble and test, and robust design. For example, while a tendon-driven joint mechanism was considered an ideal design to survive in a cold environment, a direct-drive evolutional joint mechanism was preferred for simplicity and robustness.

3.2 Northern Light Instruments

3.2.1 Northern Light Instruments

Fig. 3. Rock corer and Argus spectrometer [3] (from left to right)

The TC Corer will be supplied by Holinser and the Hong Kong Polytechnic University. Holinser is an established supplier of heritage space components. The company will supply a corer (mass approximately 400g) capable of boring up to 1cm into surface rocks.

3.2.2 Argus Spectrometer

The spectrometer proposed for the Northern Light mission is Argus 4000, based on the Argus 1000 spectrometer. The Argus 1000 (shown in Fig. 3) was originally developed at York University for Earth observation and is currently in operation as part of the Canadian CanX-2 mission, launched in 2008 on an Indian Polar Satellite Launch Vehicle (PSLV).

The Argus 4000 includes up to four independent spectrometer elements. The front-end optics will be developed to interface the spectrometers and to separate the diffuse and direct radiation components of the Martian atmosphere.

3.2.3 Wide Field-of-View Camera

Two types of cameras are currently considered for the Northern Light mission: narrow and wide field-of-view cameras. The wide field camera will provide an overall color view of the lander's surroundings. This view will be used for an initial assessment of the landing site and will help to plan rover deployment and route planning. This camera will open the first Canadian window into Mars, which should be of great interest to the media and the public.

3.2.4 Narrow Field-of-View Camera

The narrow field camera will provide a very high resolution, panoramic view of the landing site. Color filters will perform spectral mapping and mineral identification; the camera will also perform limited atmospheric and astronomical observations. The Earth as seen from Mars will be between 7 and 50 arc-seconds in size; it will therefore be possible to capture an "Earth rise" with the narrow field camera.

3.2.5 Other Instruments on the Lander or the Rover

Several other instruments are also currently considered in addition to the crucial tools discussed above. Many of these instruments will be directly mounted on the lander or on the rovers. The following is just a short list of the possible instruments:

- **Aurora spectrometer:** a small, geological spectrometer optimized for the surface exploration of Mars.
- **Environmental sensors:** to measure UV, oxidizing substances, air temperature, air pressure, wind speed, dust impact and vibration.
- **Mars Active Seismic Surveyor (MASSur):** led by Robert Stewart at GENNIX Technology Corp. and University of Calgary
- **Ground-penetrating radar (GPR)**: to get localized subsurface mapping

3.3 Design Concepts

The proposed 4-DOF configuration provides sufficient positioning capability required for the Northern Light measurement tasks. It provides the dexterity and accuracy required for placing the drill onto rock and soil samples within its vicinity.

In [4], the design concept of a prototype manipulation system onboard Rocky 7 is described in detail. In the article, it shows how most of Mars exploration can be achieved with four degrees of freedom, with the exception of access to horizontal utility tray, which require additional degrees of freedom. The proposed 4-DOF design with a passive DOF to erect the manipulator from the stowed to deployed configurations (shown in Fig. 2), the arm can reach most of the areas surrounding its landing site and perform drilling operation. As pointed out in [4], the proposed configuration will not allow access to horizontal plane. However, the drilling operation does not require this specific function and was thus removed from the design.

The 4-DOFs include the waist and shoulder joint at the base, the elbow joint between the two arm segments, and a wrist joint at the distal end. The waist servo has a torque output of approximately 1480 ounce-inches. The shoulder and elbow joint servos are capable of providing a torque of about 1700 ounce-inches. The sensing and control of the robotic arm kinematic configuration is provided by external potentiometers on the servos which enable precise feedback control. The manipulator is also equipped with contact sensors at the distal end to provide tactile feedback to indicate when the arm has made an expected or unexpected contact with the ground or the lander.

The instruments are mounted at the distal end via an interface plate. A similar concept was used in the Beagle 2 position-adjustable workbench (PAW) design. In [6], the implementation of the camera system on the Beagle Paw is also described. In the paper, the authors demonstrate how the workspace of the Beagle 2 robot arm is analyzed using the images from the camera system and used for drilling and sampling. The end-effector design of the Northern Light manipulator arm employs the same concept of multi-instruments pivoted around the wrist joint.

On the interface plane attached to the wrist joint, up to two instruments can be mounted on each surface. The stereo camera, under development by the Northern Light team, will be mounted on the same side as the TC Corer. The Argus spectrometer and the second camera (for panoramic imaging) are mounted on the opposite side. In Fig. 4, only the panoramic-viewing camera and the spectrometer are shown.

4 Northern Light Manipulator System

A functional prototype manipulator has been developed at York University to demonstrate the mission concept. The details of the arm design are described in this chapter.

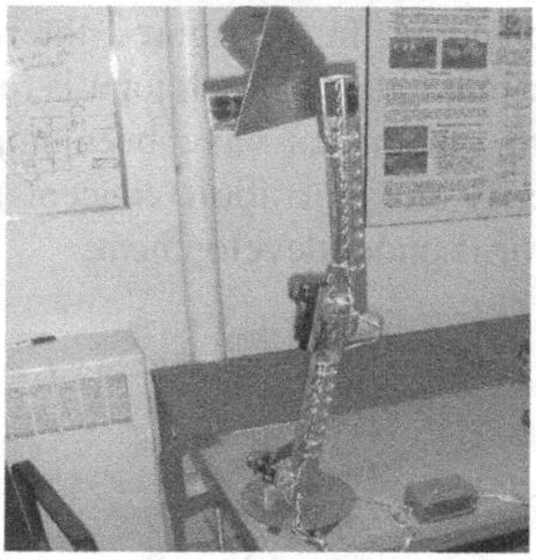

Fig. 4. Prototype of Northern Light manipulator

4.1 Joint Design

The 4-DOFs are provided by four servo motors, directly mounted at the joint. Each link measures 30 cm in length and engineered from Aluminum 6061-T651 for its light weight characteristic. The total arm weighs 1.5 kg (without the instruments). A simple narrow field-of-view camera and a spectrometer are mounted at the distal end to demonstrate the mission concept. The drilling tool is expected to arrive in late 2008 for final testing and integration.

4.2 Kinematic Analysis and Modeling

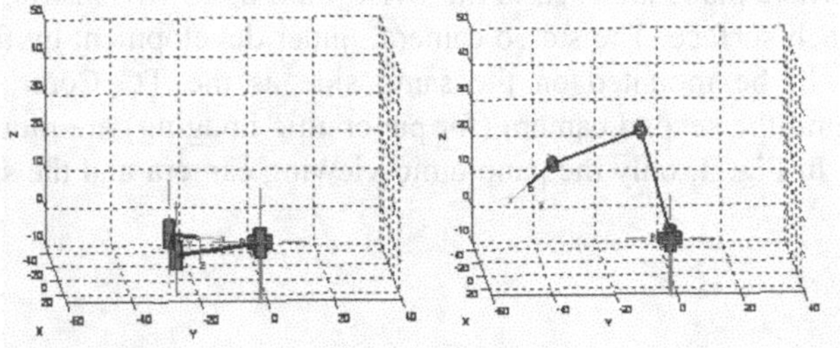

Fig. 5. Deployed and stowed arm configuration simulations

The kinematics of the proposed manipulator is examined using MATLAB simulation software. Fig. 5 shows the deployed and stowed away arm configurations (equivalent to configurations shown in Fig. 2) generated from the MATLAB simulation. In the simulation model, each link is 30 cm in length (as in the prototype arm) with four degrees of freedom. In the figures, the red vertical bar represents the mounting position of the manipulator. Each joint is represented by a blue dot.

The inverse and forward kinematics have been implemented in MATLAB. Simulation software to verify the operation concept and also to analyze the workspace of the manipulator is under development.

4.3 Control Design

Each servo motor in the prototype is driven independently using off-the-shelf hardware. In the final design, we have proposed to develop a customized joint control system in order to meet the mass, power and volume constraints. Note that not only is the power limited to 2 Watts in nominal operation (with peak of 10 Watts for short period of time), the electronics need to survive the extreme temperatures of the Martian environment. The prototype design is based on a simple position control with serial interface to the host computer. The power to each servo motor is supplied through the controller with an arbitrary maximum current of 1 A. In the final design, the pulse-width-modulation signal created by H-bridges, controlled from the microprocessor, will be implemented.

A similar design is also proposed for the motor control in the Northern Light micro-rover system. By implementing consistent design throughout the mission, we aim to reduce the development cost and schedule to the minimum level. In the proposed design, an ARM9 based microprocessor is proposed. As a development tool a Linuxstamp development board was selected to support the engineering process. The Linuxstamp is an open source processor module based on the Atmel AT91RM9200 microcontroller. Development can be done over Ethernet using SSH, or directly by using the USB device port which is connected via an FT232 USB/serial chip to the debug serial port on the AT91RM9200.

The mission operation is planned in a flow-chart manner with if-then statements to identify as many foreseeable events (such as obstacles or failure to drill) as possible. The objective is to maximize the local intelligence to avoid the delay in operation due to the communication between human operation on Earth and the manipulator on Mars.

The goal is to create a manipulator that will intelligently and robustly navigate itself to a rock or soil sample and perform scientific experiments in a single communication cycle. Based on the initial images from the camera, ground control decides on a target and uploads commands with conditional statements. Then a statistical expectation-maximization algorithm helps the manipulator vision system segment the target rock from the background. Using a 3-D model of the target, the desired final pose of the end-effector is selected. Once the manipulator has made contact, it moves back slightly to re-image the target. After taking measurements, the manipulator returns to its homing position, transmits status and sensor information, and awaits further commands.

Since mission operations must be performed using only a single command cycle, the on-board software of the manipulator must be robust and versatile to handle various situations and failures. Therefore, the software has to make intelligent decisions in real-time through reasoning. The current approach is to plan off-board in combination with on-board execution. Off-board planning is realized by a contingency planner using the 3-D models of the environment and target to generate execution plans with contingencies to deal with anticipated failures based on the approach in [12]. These plans are checked via simulation. On-board execution involves a robust sequence execution engine which can handle multitasking, time constraints, contingency plan selection, and floating plans of contingencies.

5 Integration and Testing

Based on the prototype design described here, the Northern Light team is preparing to assemble and test a flight model of the manipulator. The flight model of the Northern Light Manipulator hardware and control electronics will be validated for space flight at York University's Space Test Facility within the Centre for Research in Earth & Space Science (CRESS). The CRESS facilities include a thermal-vacuum chamber, two clean rooms, and a vibration tester. The thermal-vacuum chamber is 1.5 m in diameter, and replicates vacuum conditions via the use of closed cycle helium cryo-pumps and oil-less vacuum pumps. The chamber is capable of duplicating the temperature extremes faced in space, by cycling through a range of -140°C (-220°F) to 140°C (284°F). Temperature data acquisition and control is through a dedicated PC. The Class 10,000 clean room allows for safer handling and assembly of high precision and often delicate spacecraft components. The vibration test facility is a Dynamics Solutions DS-3300/12-15 shaker system. The shaker has a 1500 kgf rating and 51 mm maximum displacement.

The Northern Light mission will be operated mainly by Thoth's Space Tracking and Navigation (STN) division. STN uses telecommunications assets in Canada and around the world to offer specialist space-tracking and communications services with near-Earth and interplanetary spacecraft. Thoth operates the Algonquin Radio Observatory (ARO) providing geodetic services and deep space network communications utilizing the 46 m antenna. The 46 m (150 ft) antenna at Algonquin Radio Observatory is Canada's largest antenna. Commissioned in 1965, the telescope is a fine example of a monster machine. The giant dish is fully steerable and can track with arc second precision the faintest object in the sky. Powerful motors turn the giant antenna in azimuth and elevation to point at any location in the sky. The moving part of the antenna rests 1000 tons on the pedestal base.

6 Conclusion

In the paper, we reviewed the design constraints on the Northern Light Manipulator system proposed for the Mars exploration and drilling operations. The prototype manipulator for the proposed mission was developed at York University to demonstrate the engineering constraints and operational concepts. Currently, only the camera and spectrometer are mounted at the distal end of the 60 cm manipulator system. The plan to extend the design to include the TC Corer and a second camera is also proposed. The flight model of the manipulator system will also feature the customized electronics with force feedback and temperature control.

The Northern Light mission is currently undergoing sub-system level design and the system level integration is planned for early 2009. The team is aiming to complete the environmental testing by 2010 to prepare for launch as early as 2011.

References

[1] Quine, B.. R. Lee, C. Roberts and the Northern Light Team (2008). "Northern Light – A Canadian Mars Lander: Development Plan." Canadian Aeronautics & Space Institute ASTRO 2008 Conference, April 2008.

[2] Doyon, M, et al., "The SPDM Task Verification Facility: On the Dynamic Emulation in One-g Environment using Hardware-in-the-Loop Simulation, "Proceeding of the 7th International Symposium on Artificial Intelligence, Robotics and Automation in Space:
i-SAIRAS 2003, NARA, Japan, May 19-23, 2003.

[3] Spectrometer IR 900 nm to 1700 nm - Argus 1000 Infrared Spectrometers, Thoth Technology website: http://www.thoth.ca/spectrometers.htm

[4] Richard Volpe, Timothy Ohm, Richard Petras, Richard Welch, J., "A Prototype Manipulation System for Mars Rover Science Operations," Published in proceedings of IEEE□RSJ International Conference on Intelligent Robots and Systems (IROS97), Grenoble, France, Setember 7-11 1997. also presented at the International Conference on Mobile and Planetary Robots, Santa Monica CA, Jan. 29-Feb. 1 1997.

[5] The Internet Encyclopedia of Science, Beagle 2 on the website http://www.daviddarling.info/encyclopedia/B/Beagle2.html

[6] A.D. Griffiths et al., "The Scientific objectives of the Beagle 2 stero camera system," Lunar and Planetary Science Conference, Houston, Texas March 17-21, 2003.

Design and Application of GeoNet System for ABC Cooperative Environment

TaeMin Kim[1], JinWoo Choi[1], Myung-Kyu Yi[1], and Young-Kyu Yang[1]

[1] Dept of computer Science, Kyung-won University, KyungKi-Do 461-701, Korea
{scc0309, cjw49, kainos, ykyang}@kyungwon.ac.kr

Abstract. The Atmospheric Brown Cloud (ABC) project is an international research effort initiated by the United Nations Environment Program (UNEP). However, lack of cooperative application system for the collected ground measurement data from ABC observatories, prevents intimate cooperative studies among the researchers. In our proposal, therefore, we establish an e-Science based cooperative web environment called GeoNet(Global Earth Observation Network) so that ABC scientists can effectively share and utilize the ABC data. Therefore, ABC scientists can share and manage more effectively satellite images from various satellites and collected ground measurement data from ABC observatories through GeoNet.

1 Introduction

The Korea lies in the northeastern part of the Asian continent so that the climate of the Korean Peninsula is affected a lot by the fine particles flown from dessert and industrial area in China[1]. The Atmospheric Brown Cloud (ABC) discovered in 1999 is a large scale atmospheric haze produced when chemical compounds in the air are adsorbed onto the cloud condensation nuclei or cloud particles. The ABC is an air pollution phenomenon which scatters the radiation from the sun and forms a large brownish haze layer. The thickness of the brown cloud reaches from a few kilometers to a few hundreds kilometers. ABC usually occurs in Southeast Asia where the population density is high, the source of aerosol and greenhouse gas is widespread and rapid industrialization is under way. The South Asian haze is analyzed to be caused by the yellow sand and smoke pollution from China. ABCs reduce the solar radiation, which lowers the temperature of the earth, evaporation of seawater and precipitation, reducing the agricultural products. Recently, an international cooperative observation of ABC is being carried out under UNEP (United Nations Environment Program) in order to observe the generation of ABC and its effect on weather change[2]. Observation facilities are installed for ABC at

O.-H. Byeon et al. (eds.), *Future Application and Middleware Technology on e-Science*,
DOI 10.1007/978-1-4419-1719-5_5, © Springer Science+Business Media, LLC 2010

Korea Climate Observatory - Gosan (KCO-G)[3]. Through such international cooperative observation in supersites in Asia, ABC scientists make an effort for the calibration of equipment and information exchange of ABC. However, lack of cooperative application system for the collected ground measurement data from ABC observatories including KCO-G, prevents intimate cooperative studies among the researchers. In our proposal, therefore, we establish an e-Science based cooperative web environment called GeoNet(Global Earth Observation Network) so that ABC scientists can effectively share and utilize the ABC data. Therefore, ABC scientists can share and manage more effectively satellite images from various satellites and collected ground measurement data from ABC observatories through GeoNet.

2 Design of GeoNet system

2.1 The structure of GeoNet system

Fig. 1 shows the structure of the GeoNet system consisted of 5 layers. The high 2 layers are customized for cooperative environment of the ABC scientists. This database is constructed by collected the ground measurement data related with ABC through the nodes scattered in the GeoNet. GeoNet portal facilitates user's access to the remotely scattered sites. Moreover, GeoNet portal has been developed using the GridSphere framework, which implements the portlet architecture and is compatible with the JSR168, or Portlet API, standard. Portlet consists of core portlet and application portlet. In core portlet log-in, lot-out, data registration, and data search can be supported for ABC scientists.

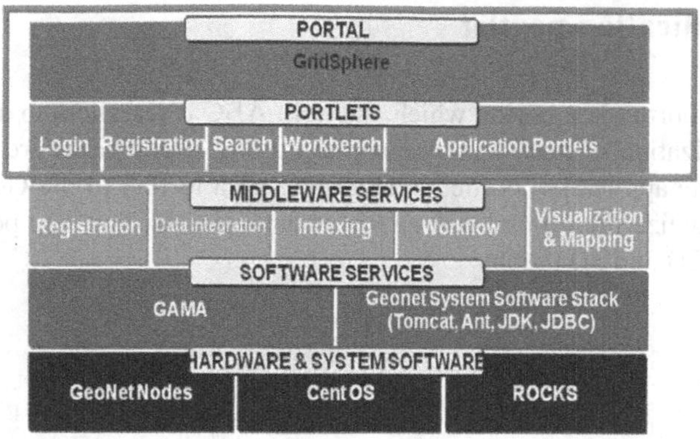

Fig. 1. Structure of the GeoNet system

2.1.1 Core Portlet

The functions supported by core portlet are as follows.

- User Management: Login and logout are provided to the ABC researchers. Selection of languages in portal, account management, group management, and information correction of the user profile such as names and e-mails are supported.
- Role Management: Managing the access authorities of the ABC researcher's portlet is provided. The GeoNet portal administrator can set up the access authorities of the ABC researcher's portlet, and ABC researchers can access to the portlet and resources according to the established authorities.
- Layout Management: Provide layout functions for the convenience of the ABC researchers. The accessible portlet can be activated and deactivated. Allow the portlet arrangement when the users want.
- Data Management: Provide functions of data resource management for co-operative research of ABC scientist. ABC researchers can register, edit and remove their ground measurement data of ABC. Provide a search function so that ABC researchers can approach data that others have registered as well as his own.

2.1.2 Application portlet

Application portlet is a portlet which can help ABC researchers to analyzed ABC data. Visualization of data, data preprocessing and applications are also included in it. Now the application portlet is devising a plan to link to the Google Earth in order to visualize the ground measurement data. It also develops portlet that can visualize in 2D and 3D graphs.

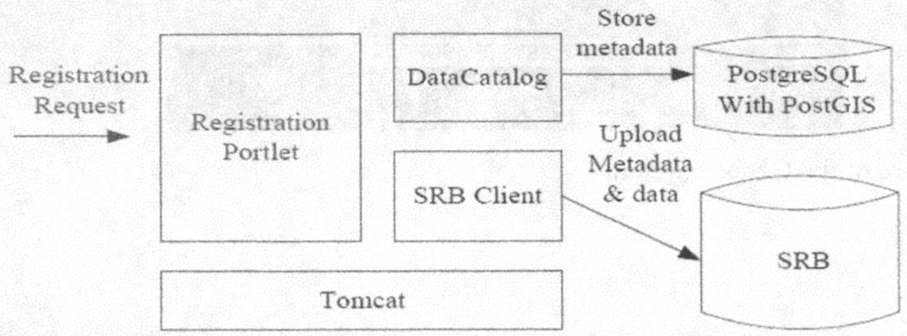

Fig. 2. System flow for registration

2.1.3 Middleware Service

GeoNet provides a middleware service between resource and application users. The middleware service provides such functions as below.

- Registration : In order to be registered, users have to register metadata, schema data and data item. The registration of data is processed through registration portlet provided from the portal.
- Data Integration: Various unification functions are provided for the registered schema and data items. Such function is provided through MyWorkbench menu in the portal.
- Indexing: Tex indexing function is provided for metadata. ABC scientists can use the search function based on text in the portal.
- Workflow: Kepler workflow system can be used to control some of the processing behind-the-scenes.

2.1.4 Visualization & Mapping

Mapping and visualization are provided in MyPage menu as one of the functions provided in portal.

2.1.5 Hardware & System Software

Hardware that is responsible for each function can be comprised of one or many hardware. It can be constituted in a scattered environment.

2.2 Data registration and search resources

The data registration in GeoNet is a service offered when users provides his data to other users. Fig. 3 shows a system flow for registration and components need for application. First ABC users submit their data using the registration portlet. Then the Tomcat[4] based portlet generates metadata, which are stored in the PostGIS[5] based PostgreSQL database, and the metadata produced in SRB for mass storage application and data provided by users are stored. This enhances the efficiency of data search and enables the efficient use of mass storage equipment.

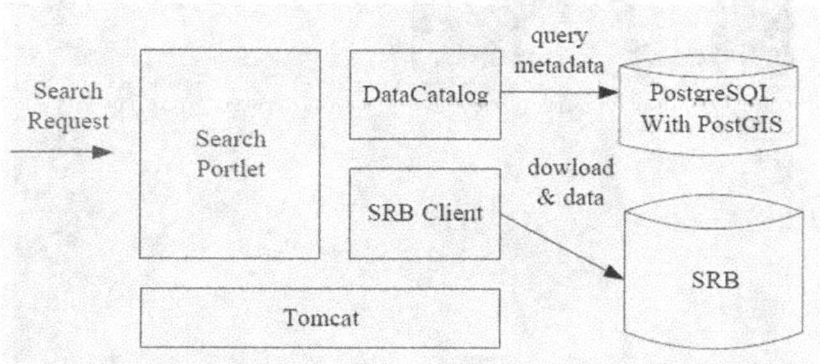

Fig. 3. System flow for search

Fig. 3 shows the system flow for search resources process in GeoNet and the related system components. Users can send the search conditions using the GeoNet Search Page menu. DataCatalog service helps users to find confirmed data from the metadata where a search condition has been stored. The search results include the location information in the scattered mass storages as well as required data. Required data are downloaded based on site information in the storage.

3 Application

This study draws out a use-case scenario so that ABC researchers can utilize in their own application fields, which is linked to GeoNet platform so that people can work under cooperative environment. The application part can be categorized into modeling-analysis and visualization parts.

3.1 Modeling-analysis part

In the modeling-analysis part, models for visualizing ground measurement data are analyzed. To analysis for ABC, the ground measured data can be selected according to time and observation factors. In the case of satellite image data, MODIS satellite data are analyzed so that observed data for Normalized Difference Vegetation Index (NDVI) and Aerosol Optical Depth (AOD) are extracted for visualization and assimilation with the ground measurement data.

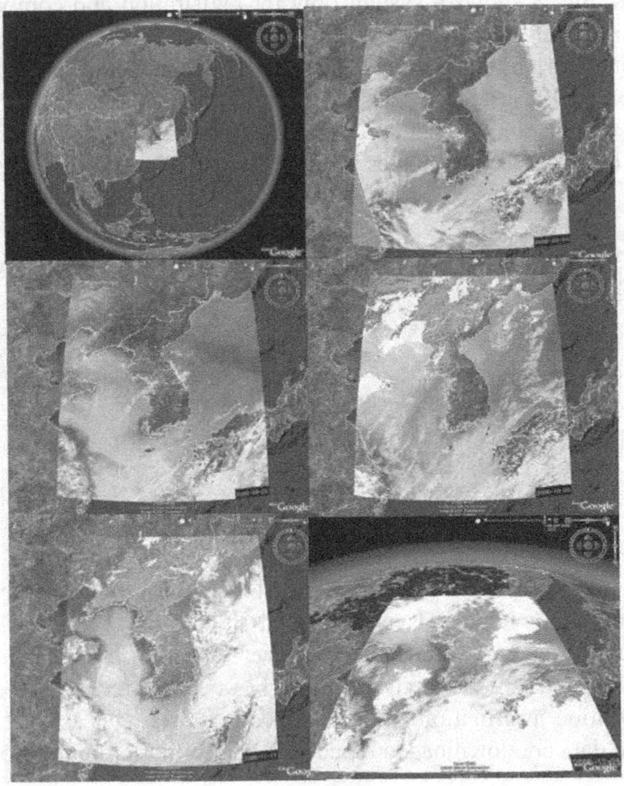

Fig. 4. NDVI analyzed results of the MODIS satellite images

3.2 Visualization part

Visualization parts studies visualization method of vector data for expressing the weather variables such as National Centers for Environmental Prediction/ National Center for Atmospheric Research (NCEP/NCAR) reanalysis wind fields into graphs. These can be expressed as simulation together with measured values that have been extracted from satellite data analysis. Fig. 4 shows the NDVI analyzed results of the MODIS satellite images from September of 2007 to December of 2007 by linking to Google Earth using Google Earth's tag-based Keyhole Mark-up Language(KML) formant. Fig. 5 shows the visualization example of Aerosol Optical Depth (AOD) and wind filed (850 hPa). Recently as the plug-in and JavaScript are publicized so that they can be easily be operated on Google Earth, Google Earth can be directly utilized for GeoNet application portlet. In order to for the ABC researchers to share the easy public ownership of the observed data such as aerosol, Lidar, and analyzed results though GeoNet in the future, the application service will be widened starting from where the need is larger.

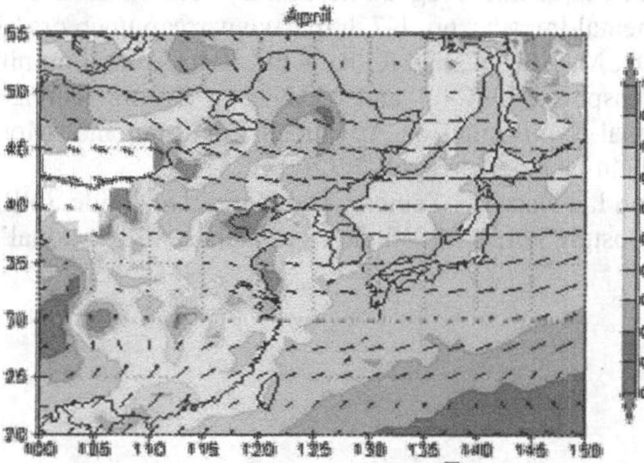

Fig. 5. Visualization example of AOD and wind filed

4 Conclusion

The purpose of our research is to establish cooperative web environment called GeoNet and to devolpe the novel meteorological service that provides increase in research efficiency and positive synergy effect in related research fields. To do so, our strategy are as follows. First at the early stage based on the ABC data from Korea Climate Observatory Gosan, data are collected. Second GeoNet system were designed for managing the data and the ABC users. Third, modelling and analysis were carried out in order to utilize the satellite image data and ground measurement data. Finally, visualization method was studied in order to efficiently represent theses data. The techniques for java based preprocessing of the satellite images and Google Earth based vector data visualization were implemented. Therefore, the cooperative web environment developed by our study will be serviced that provides ABC user community for discussion of experimental results and analysis along with sharing and managing of ground measurement data and satellite images.

References

1. Choi. J.-C., M. Lee, Y. Chun, J. Kim, and S.-N. Oh : Chemical composition and source signature of spring aerosol in Seoul, Korea, J. Geophys. Res.- Atmosphere, 106, D16, 18,067-18,074(2001).
2. United Nations Environmental Programme(UNEP) : The Asian Brown Cloud : Climate and Other Environmental Impacts, pp. 1-7, http://www.rrcap.unep.org/abc/pub.cfm (2002)
3. Kim, J., S.-N. Oh, M.-K. Park, and K.-R., Kim : Background monitoring and long-range transport of atmospheric CFC-11 and CFC-12 at Kosan, Korea, Proceedings on The Third International Symposium on Advanced Environmental Monitoring, October 31-November 2, Cheju Island, Korea, 69-72(2002).
4. Jason Brittain and Ian Darwin : Tomcat: The Definitive Guide, O'Reilly (2007)
5. Richard Blum: PostgreSQL 8 for Windows (Database Professional's Library), McGraw-Hill (2007)

Application Architecture of Avian Influenza Research Collaboration Network in Korea e-Science

Hoon Choi, JuneHawk Lee

Korea Institute of Science and Technology Information

choid@kisti.re.kr, juneh@kisti.re.kr

Abstract In the pursuit of globalization of the AI e-Science environment, KISTI is fostering to extend the AI research community to the AI research institutes of neighboring countries and to share the AI e-Science environment with them in the near future. In this paper we introduce the application architecture of AI research collaboration network (AIRCoN). AIRCoN is a global e-Science environment for AI research conducted by KISTI. It consists of AI virus sequence information sharing system for sufficing data requirement of research community, integrated analysis environment for analyzing the mutation pattern of AI viruses and their risks, epidemic modeling and simulation environment for establishing national effective readiness strategy against AI pandemics, and knowledge portal for sharing expertise of epidemic study and unpublished research results with community members.

1 Introduction

Avian Influenza (AI) is a deadly infectious disease caused by viruses adapted to birds. Since the viruses in birds can mutate to easily infect humans, the disease concerns to humans, who have no immunity against it. Historically AI viruses infected pigs and mixed with pig influenza viruses. The two types of viruses exchanged their genetic information and reproduced a new type of viruses that could infect humans and spread from people to people. Previous influenza pandemics have started this way.

Outbreak of AI is closely related to migration routes of birds and frequent travels of human beings. Effective readiness against AI pandemics depends on the success of international collaboration efforts. In particular, the epidemic pattern of AI virus in Korea is similar to that in the countries of Northeast and Southeast Asia such as China, Japan, Mongol, Vietnam, and so on. Thus, AI researchers in

O.-H. Byeon et al. (eds.), *Future Application and Middleware Technology on e-Science*,
DOI 10.1007/978-1-4419-1719-5_6, © Springer Science+Business Media, LLC 2010

Korea strive to collaborate with government research agencies of these neighboring countries to establish nation-wide effective readiness strategy for AI pandemics.

In support of their efforts, KISTI is developing a global AI e-Science environment to alleviate the temporal and spatial barrier to AI research collaboration among those countries and to enhance their productivity. KISTI has organized AI research community including KCDC(Korea Center for Disease Control), NVRQS(National Veterinary Research and Quarantine Service), many universities in Korea and University of Tuebingen in Germany. In the pursuit of globalization of the AI e-Science environment, KISTI is fostering to extend the AI research community to the AI research institutes of neighboring countries and to share the AI e-Science environment with them in the near future.

As the development of AI e-Science environment is currently in the beginning stage, KISTI and AI research community are under construction of essential core services like AI virus sequence information sharing and epidemic modeling and simulation. They also are planning value-added services like knowledge portal, which enable the community to make use of experts' experimental results and enhance AI research productivity.

In this paper we introduce the application architecture of AI research collaboration network (AIRCoN). AIRCoN is a global e-Science environment for AI research conducted by KISTI. It consists of AI virus sequence information sharing system for sufficing data requirement of research community, integrated analysis environment for analyzing the mutation pattern of AI viruses and their risks, epidemic modeling and simulation environment for establishing national effective readiness strategy against AI pandemics, and knowledge portal for sharing expertise of epidemic study and unpublished research results with community members.

The remainder of this paper is as follows. Section 2 introduces some activities related to our project. Section 3 outlines the requirement of AIRCoN gathered from research community including KCDC and NVRQS. Section 4 provides a description of application architecture of AIRCoN and its major components. Section 5 concludes.

2. Related Works

Avian Flu Grid (AFG) is a global project to collaborate AI research among Grid computing research community in Asia-Pacific Rim[1]. AFG focuses on computing the conformations of N1 by use of MD simulation techniques, and discovery of new drugs based on the conformations[2]. AFG is also interested in data sharing and epidemic simulation.

There have been several sites for sharing Influenza virus information such as BioHealthBase[4] of Bioinformatics Resource Center, Influenza Sequence

Database(ISD) of Los Alamos National Laboratory (LANL)[5], Influenza Virus Resource of NCBI[6], Influenza sequence and epitope database (ISED)[7] of KCDC, to name a few. The sites copy AI virus information from public data sources, store it in a separate DB and service it to Influenza researchers. However, they do not support integrated search functionalities like a federated search.

While Influenza researchers publish only a small part of AI gene sequences, they store most of the information in their own private DBs. To improve reliability and accuracy of research results, they need to integrate the private DBs as well as public DBs. AIRCoN provides services of virtual data integration of private DBs and epidemic simulation [3], to promote sharing of AI virus information.

3. Requirement

To collect the requirements for application architecture of AIRCoN, we have organized a global AI e-Science community whose members are KCDC, NVRQS, University of Tuebingen, SNU, KAIST and KISTI. Through the interview with them, we have defined the requirements as follows.

- Sharing AI virus sequence information for global collaboration of AI research
  - KCDC, NVRQS, veterinary colleges in Korea want to share AI virus information among them. Information sharing enhances the performance of their research efforts in analyzing patterns of AI virus mutation and developing diagnostic kits and anti-viral drug.
  - Since the patterns of virus mutation occurring in Korea is very similar to those in China, Japan, Mongol and Vietnam, the government research agencies in Korea require AI virus information to be exchanged with those neighbor countries. They strive for international collaborative activities to share the information with one another and improve effectiveness of their national public health programs.
  - To promote these efforts, the community preferentially requires the development of a data integration system to support sharing AI virus sequence information among the government research agencies in Korea. The data integration system will be globalized to integrate AI information owned by the research institutes of neighbor countries in northeast and southeast Asia.

- Utilization of sharable bioinformatics software and computing resource for AI research community
  - NIH of KCDC collects human and avian influenza virus information from local branch offices in Korea. They analyze genomic and proteomic

analysis to predict mutation and risk of AI viruses and prepare public health programs for readiness against pandemics.
  - NVRQS operate a national surveillance network to take preventive measures against outbreak of AI and to prepare a rapid containment strategy for minimizing the amount of damage in livestock farming industry. They analyze AI virus gene sequences from infected migratory birds and poultry of farms all year round, and isolate the possibility of infecting human beings.
  - AI e-Science community requires computing resource and various bio-informatics software to accomplish their research results. The bioinformatics tools are used for sequence analysis, mutation prediction, expression analysis, protein structure prediction, protein interaction analysis, protein docking etc.

- Establishing effective readiness strategies against AI pandemics
  - Based on WHO recommendation, KCDC assume AI pandemic scenarios that most likely take place, and prepare progressive readiness plans to minimize the amount of social and economical damage.
  - KCDC are struggling to study epidemic modeling and simulation with insufficient manpower and computing infrastructure. They want to prepare effective readiness against AI pandemics by the use of mathematical models that reflect the regional and demographic properties in Korea, the possibility of AI dissemination in metro cities by people-to-people contacts, and so on.
  - KCDC require a visual epidemic modeling and simulation research environment to establish sophisticate strategies of preventive measures against AI pandemics, on a level with advanced countries like USA, UK, Japan, and Germany.

- Cyberspace for sharing experimental knowledge within AI research community
  - Scientists frequently use Internet space to share their expertise experimental knowledge and new scientific discovery with each other.
  - AI e-Science community wants to keep a cyber space for sharing the details of experience such as *in silico* experiments and research memos with other members of community. This will help novice researchers enhance their research productivity to the level of experienced researchers.
  - The community needs an effective way of sharing knowledge so that community members can organize knowledge into a knowledge base with taxonomies or ontologies. They also want to navigate and search the knowledge base.

4. AIRCoN Architecture

Application architecture of AIRCoN that has been derived from the requirements of AI e-Science community is depicted in the figure 4-1. Four major components of AIRCoN are AI virus sequence information integration system for sharing disparate data sources and sufficing data requirement of AI research, integrated analysis environment for analyzing the mutation pattern of AI viruses and their risks, epidemic modeling and simulation environment for establishing national effective readiness strategy against AI pandemics, and a knowledge portal system for sharing expertise of epidemic study and unpublished research results with community members.

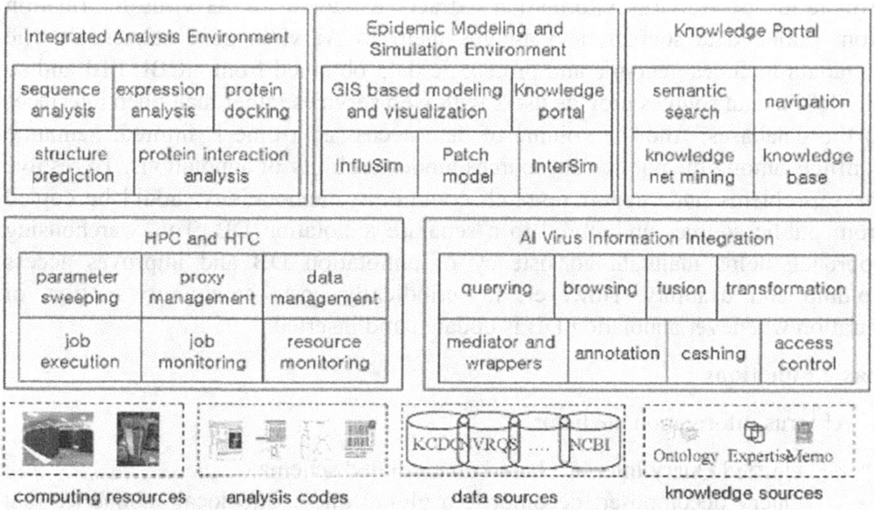

Fig. 1. Application architecture of AIRCoN

4.1 AI virus sequence information integration system

The purpose of AI virus information integration system (AVIS) is to realize sharing of information related to AI virus research with AI e-Science community. The scope of AVIS includes AI virus genomic and proteomic information owned by stakeholders such as KCDC, NVRQS and university institutes in Korea. With AVIS, authorized users can access AI virus information from disparate data sources. AVIS annotates AI virus sequences with semantic metadata from public data sources. Thereby, AVIS creates value-added information to enhance the research productivity of AI e-Science community.

Approach

- Mediation approach to integration of AI virus information

Data sources of AI genomic and proteomic information of stakeholders in Korea is virtually integrated by the use of mediator and wrappers. The mediation approach [8] enables users to access data related to their research from disparate and distributed data sources without intrusion of system management policy of the stakeholders. Different from warehousing approach, mediation approach guarantees autonomy of data sources and improve up-to-date accessibility of data contents.

- Warehousing approach to annotating AI virus information

Annotation of AI virus information extracts metadata for AI virus information from public data sources, and assigns them to AI virus gene sequences. The metadata includes genomic and proteomic data obtained from NCBI, EBI and so on. Public data sources provide users with web services rather than open interfaces to the databases. And the volume of data access at a time is limited. Semantic conflicts among the public data sources hinder usability of annotations. To resolve these problems and support research community, annotations should be copied from public sources and stored to a separate annotation DB. This warehousing approach helps maintain consistency of annotation DB and improves access volume and usability. However, it periodically costs community's effort of curation whenever annotation DB is updated and inserted.

Basic Functions

- AI virus information mediator
  - Unified Query Interface based on mediated schema
  - Query decomposer: decompose a global query into local subqueries that can be processed in local data sources.
  - Subquery fuser: synthesize the results from local data sources to a single table
  - Wrapper: transform a subquery to a local query executable on a data source, and transform the results of a local query to the results of a subquery based on a mediated schema

- Annotation DB for AI virus information
  - Standard taxonomies and ontologies for annotations
  - Annotation ETL(Extraction, Transformation & Load)
  - Curation interface for scientists

4.2 Integrated analysis environment for AI research

Integrated analysis environment (IAE) purposes to provide AI community with a unified interface for collecting and analyzing AI related data. The unified interface is connected to AVIS and can be used to collect AI related data from disparate data sources. The environment supports bioinformatics open source codes and community's in-house codes. It supports large scale computing facilities to run the analysis codes for AI research. The analysis codes includes commercial programs as well as libraries for protein docking, structure prediction, expression analysis, sequence analysis, protein interaction analysis and so on.

Approach

- Development of IAE with customizable user interface for AI genomic and proteomic study

IAE improves user convenience by supporting a customizable interface suited to objectives of data analysis. The customizable interface is implemented with the eclipse rich client platform [9]. The rich client platform enables a user to extend analysis services for querying and analyzing AI related data to new applications by developing plug-ins for them. Thereby, a user can easily implement his research environment composed of analysis and data services for his research problems.

- Support of large scale computing resources and external data sources

Bioinformatics tools for analyzing AI virus information mostly require the access to multiple data sources and large scale computing resources to complete genomic and proteomic analysis. To meet the computing requirement, the integrated analysis environment provides high performance resources like clusters and supercomputers by the use of Grid computing technology. With the computing resources, AI researchers get more reliable results with ease on right time.

- Supporting open source code software for AI virus research

AI virus research requires the bioinformatics software to do phylogenetic analysis, protein structure analysis. In bioinformatics, analytical software and API such as BioJava, BioPerl, BioPython has been developed, widely accepted and deployed. The integrated analysis environment is under development to support AI community with a variety of analysis techniques by assembling the open source code libraries.

Basic Functions

- Protein docking service
- Structure prediction service
- Expression analysis service
- Sequence analysis service

- Protein interaction analysis service
- Data collection and analysis service

4.3 AI epidemic modeling and simulation environment

AI epidemic modeling and simulation environment provides the modeling and concrete and reliable basic data for establishing the effective readiness against AI pandemics. The basic data is created by applying InfluSim and InterSim [3] modified to reflect demographic, geographic and climate properties of Korea. From the epidemic simulation, researchers can prepare the rapid containment and intervention strategies to minimize the national damage.

Approach

- Development of AI/PI epidemic modeling and simulation software based on mathematical models

KISTI and KCDC collaborate with University of Tuebingen to acquire the capabilities of epidemic modeling and simulation software, InfluSim and InterSim. We develop simulation models and software suited for the properties in Korea by analyzing sensitivity of parameters. InfluSim is based on deterministic mathematical model, and InterSim is on stochastic network model.

Basic Functions

- AI epidemic modeling and simulation service
  - GUI based epidemic modeling tools
  - Execution environment of epidemic simulation software
  - GIS based visualization of simulation results
  - knowledge sharing for epidemic modeling

4.4 Knowledge Portal for Knowledge Sharing

The purpose of this component is to develop a knowledge portal system to promote collaboration activities within AI e-Science community. The system provides AI community with a cyber space to collaborate and maximizes the opportunities of new scientific discovery by sharing knowledge among community members.

Knowledge dealt in the portal system is categorized as follows.

- Expertise of experienced researchers: *in silico* experiments and their results

- Research output: papers, intellectual properties, technical reports, research notes, memos, etc.
- Record of collaborative interactions within community

Approach

- Knowledge management focusing on semantic associations.

To give users a unified view, knowledge management focuses on the semantic associations of knowledge objects. The scope of knowledge objects covers common research issues of community, collaborative activities on the issues, and the results of collaboration. Knowledge objects are organized according to parts of standard biomedical ontologies. Knowledge portal provides semantic search and navigation services based on the ontologies, and improves the utilization of knowledge.

- Monitoring collaborative activities within community

Knowledge portal requires monitoring functionality to promote the collaborations within AI e-Science community. To monitor the collaborations, cross-reference relationships between the community members and the knowledge objects are collected and analyzed. The analysis of the cross-reference information shows who works together on a specific topic, whose works are related to his work, and so on. Analysis of the cross-reference information is completed with a data mining technique.

Basic Functions

- Knowledge portal service
  - ontology storage and retrieval
  - semantics based knowledge retrieval and navigation
  - knowledge network mining
  - generation of association data
  - community activity monitoring

5. Summary and Future Research

KISTI and government research agencies in Korea have been developing AI e-Science environment to provide AI community with collaborative research infrastructure. In this paper, we have proposed, AIRCoN, application architecture for AI e-Science environment, and described their major components. We focus our efforts on developing AVIS, IAE, and epidemic simulation software. The combination of AVIS and IAE is a foundation for integrating and analyzing AI virus information dispersed in public and private data sources within AI e-Science community. We are collaborating with University of Tuebingen to get the epidemic simulation software suited to the characteristics of Korea.

In near future, we will extend AI e-Science community to southeast and northeast Asian countries, and collaborate with them to prepare effective readiness against AI pandemics. To support the globalized community, AIRCoN will be extended to a global open infrastructure for AI research.

References

[1] Avian Flu Grid, http://goc.pragma-grid.net/wiki/index.php/Avian_Flu_Grid

[2] Melissa R. Landon, Rommie E. Amaro, Riccardo Baron, Chi Ho Ngan, David Ozonoff, J. Andrew McCammon and Sandor Vajda, Novel Druggable Hot Spots in Avian Influenza Neuraminidase H5N1 Revealed by Computational Solvent Mapping of a Reduced and Representative Receptor Ensemble, Chemical Biology & Drug Design, Vol. 71, Issue 2, pp. 106-116 (2008)

[3] Eichner, M, Simulation of interventions against pandemic influenza with InfluSim, Korea e-Science AHM2008, Daejeon

[4] BioHealthBase, http://biohealthbase.org

[5] Influenza Sequence database, http://www.flu.lanl.gov

[6] Influenza Virus Resource, http://www.ncbi.nlm.nih.gov/genomes/FLU/FLU.html

[7] Influenza sequence and epitope database, http://biomarker.korea.ac.kr

[8] H. Garcia-Molina , Y. Papakonstantinou , D. Quass , A. Rajaraman , Y. Sagiv , J. Ullman , V. Vassalos , J. Widom. The TSIMMIS approach to mediation: Data models and Languages. Journal of Intelligent Information Systems, 1997.

[9] Rich Client Platform, http://www.eclipse.org/articles/Article-RCP-1/tutorial1.html

York University Space Engineering Nanosatellite Demonstration (YuSend) Mission Development

Regina Lee (a), Hugh Chesser (b), Matthew Cannata (c), Ian Proper (c) and Nimal Navarathinam (c), Kartheephan Sathiyanathan (c)

Assistant Professor, Department Earth and Space Science and Engineering, PSE134 York University, 4700 Keele Street, Toronto, Ontario M3J 1P3 (416) 736-2100 ext 22095 reginal@yorku.ca

Associate Lecturer, School of Engineering, York University, 4700 Keele Street, Toronto, Ontario M3J 1P3 chesser@yorku.ca

Masters' of Science Candidates, Department Earth and Space Science and Engineering, PSE002B York University, 4700 Keele Street, Toronto, Ontario M3J 1P3 (416) 736-2100 ext 33589 mcannata@yorku.ca, hyopet@yorku.ca, nimal@yorku.ca, kingk@yorku.ca

Abstract In this paper, we review the York University Space Engineering Nanosatellite Demonstration (YuSend) program. We have identified several possible missions for CubeSat-based nanosatellites and associated enabling technologies. The potential applications for the tiny spacecraft (weighing 1kg each) include on-orbit servicing, assembly and monitoring, stereo imaging, formation flying, and GPS occultation experiments. While there are many challenges to be faced in nanosatellite design, the group is focusing on three key areas of research: power management, attitude control and autonomous mission planning. The details of current research related to the above three areas are discussed here. The objective is to demonstrate the technology to perform formation flying and on-orbit servicing using a modular power unit, thruster, and automated mission planner. This paper describes the conceptual design of York's first satellite, the YuSend-1 spacecraft. In addition, we present the spacecraft engineering facilities at York University including the space environmental test facilities and the ground station.

O.-H. Byeon et al. (eds.), *Future Application and Middleware Technology on e-Science*, DOI 10.1007/978-1-4419-1719-5_7, © Springer Science+Business Media, LLC 2010

1. Introduction

The York University Space Engineering Nanosatellite Demonstration (YuSend) program was initiated in 2007 to promote student engagement in space programs and enhance the learning experience. Several possible missions for CubeSat-based YuSend missions have been investigated and a number of mission-enabling technologies have been examined. The potential applications for tiny spacecraft (weighing 1kg each) include on-orbit servicing, assembly and monitoring, stereo imaging, formation flying, and GPS occultation experiments.

CubeSat-based nanosatellites are designed to perform a wide variety of tasks, so a modular subsystem design approach has been adopted for the YuSend platform. For each spacecraft component, the goal is to design modular, expandable, low-cost and adaptable system so that the YuSend program is developed in the most cost-effective way. While there are many possibilities for a nanosatellite design, YuSend-1 will envelope the three niche areas determined to be the most enabling technologies: power management, attitude determination and control and autonomous mission planning.

1.1 YuSend-1 System Specifications

YuSend-1 will perform three mission critical experiments: (1) image collection of the star field and transmission to the ground station, (2) orbital maneuvering using the micro-thrusters, and (3) autonomous mission planning.

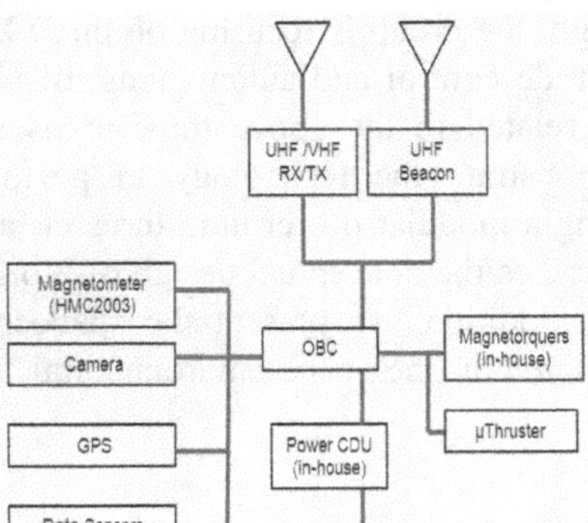

Fig. 1. YuSend-1 System Architecture

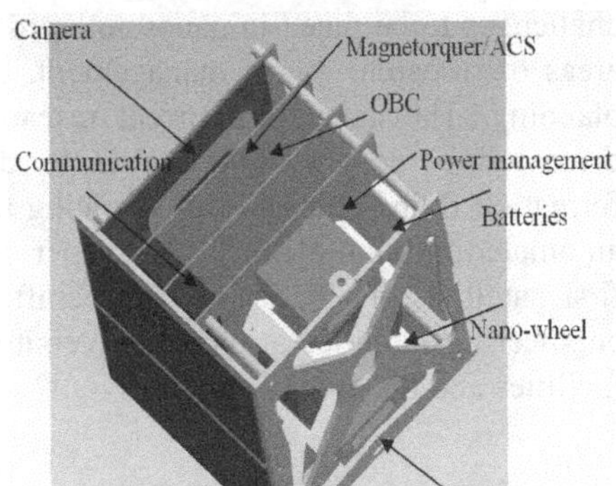

Fig. 2. Internal configuration of YusSend

1.1.1 System Architecture

The proposed YuSend-1 system architecture is shown in Fig. 1. Each subsystem will be designed around a stackable, 8 x 8cm form factor printed circuit boards. A proposed internal configuration of YuSend-1 is shown in Fig. 2. The attitude control subsystem has been laid out on a single board with interfaces to the camera, magnetorquers and attitude sensors. Likely to be adjacent to the ACS board is a customized on-board computer that provides the central processing, followed by the communication board that interfaces to the UHF/VHF antennas and UHF beacon. The power control unit is placed close to the batteries, which are mounted on opposite faces. In the center, the wheel and thrusters are mounted. Table 1 lists the envisioned modes of operation for YuSend-1 mission. It is assumed that communication to YuSend-1 is well established for each mission.

Table 1. YuSend-1 Mission Modes

Mission Modes	Task
Detumble	Slow down the tumbling motion of the spacecraft following release from the launch vehicle. The magnetometer and magnetorquers will be active during this stage.
Acquire	Acquire attitude and housekeeping information collected at 1 to 5Hz and stored. The data will be analyzed on-ground and used for qualification of the components.
Star camera demonstration	Acquire star images and store for transfer to the ground. Images taken are used for further attitude control or compressed and transferred to the ground.
Micro-thruster demonstration	Perform firing exercise of the thruster and measure the change in attitude rates. Once the thrusters are charged, the magnetorquers will release their 'hold' on the orientation and the thrusters will fire in a predetermined sequence. Once firing is complete, the star camera will take additional images to verify the changes in attitude.
Autonomous mission planning	Demonstrate the change in mission operations for potential component failures. See section 0 for more detail.

1.1.1.1 Autonomous Mission Planning Demonstration

The spacecraft will be controlled autonomously without commands from the ground station for three full orbits. During the demonstration, the system will cycle through Acquire, Camera Demonstration and Thruster demonstration missions as planned. During the second demonstration scenario, the spacecraft will execute the autonomous mission planning algorithm assuming that the critical subsystem has suffered partial loss of functionality. In Case 1 demo, three orbit demonstrations will be performed with 50 % reduction in power subsystem (loss of battery and solar cells). Case 2 demo assumes partial loss of attitude control system (failure in magnetometer, partial loss in magnetorquer functionality and unforeseen error in rate sensors). Case 3 demo is for communication system failure where the auto planner has to assume full command of the mission while attempting to establish the communication.

1.1.2 Lifetime

The lifetime of the YuSend-1 mission is 1 year from the time of release from the launch vehicle. The thruster demonstration and de-orbit demonstration will be performed only once during the mission. The camera demonstration and other subsystem qualification tests will be performed throughout its lifetime

1.1.3 Subsystems

Except for the power subsystem and attitude control subsystem, which are considered mission critical components, the other subsystems have been designed around existing technology or commercial off-the-shelf components (COTS).

1.1.3.1 Stucture

The structural subsystem has to support interfacing to the release mechanism, and may require some optimization in order that the overall spacecraft weight is less than 1kg. The nature of available release mechanisms normally restricts the external dimensions to the cubesat standard of 10x10x10cm.

The exterior structure is manufactured from aluminum 6061-T651, which is relatively inexpensive and easy to work with. Each face will be designed to accommodate body-mounted solar cells. Deployable solar panels were also briefly considered, but dropped from the YuSend-1 concept due to their complexity.

The circuit boards are stacked together to provide a stiff internal structure. The external structure encases the internal components providing sufficient strength to handle launch and handling loads, support for the solar cells and antennae and provide radiation protection. YuSend-1 will rely on a passive thermal design. The most temperature sensitive components include the batteries, which will require an environment of 0 to 40 °C during charging and -20 to 60 °C during discharging. The off-the-shelf components will be qualified in the thermal vacuum chamber before system level assembly.

1.1.3.2. On-board Computer and Software

In order to minimize design effort, an ARM9-based Linuxstamp development board was selected to support the engineering process, which has been used in other projects originating from the design team including the York University Rover. The Linuxstamp is an open source processor module based on the Atmel AT91RM9200 microcontroller. Development can be done over Ethernet using SSH, or directly by using the USB device port which is connected via an FT232 USB/serial chip to the debug serial port on the AT91RM9200.

Following the successful completion of the software development and component testing, a purpose-built board will be designed for the specific goals of the mission. The board will be laid out to fit on the required form factor, and space use considerations such as part selection and power efficiency may necessitate some design modification.

Currently it is assumed that the protocol for data exchange will be based on asynchronous serial transmission. The OBC will maintain real-time communication in order to execute real-time commands and store data with time stamps. During the majority of the spacecraft lifetime, the OBC shall collect the health and housekeeping data from each subsystem and forward it to the ground station. Minimum data storage (size to be determined) is also required in order to maintain the mission critical data until the next communication opportunity is available.

The test software is developed in C using Linux as the operating system; this allows flexibility in both development and troubleshooting. Further investigation is planned to determine the optimal operating system for the proposed mission. The RedHat eCos Linux distribution, for example, may be considered for its small memory footprint and larger developer base. Also, community ports of uClibc-based distributions such as uClinux can provide drivers and a reliable code base for customizing the OS to better fit the specific needs of the mission.

1.1.3.3 Communications

Based on a recent survey of cubesat communications performance [4], our approach will be to use commercially available onboard radio components. Our group has been in touch with the GENSO organization (General Educational Network for Satellite Operations) and is currently assembling a ground station to participate in the ground station network. Adhering to this communications standard should allow our mission to benefit from this excellent university-based space mission initiative for improved communications reliability and throughput.

1.2 YuSend-1 Power System

1.2.1 Critical Component Design

Emerging technologies in the consumer world provide the potential for a very cost effective and miniaturized Electrical Power System (EPS) by utilizing COTS components. Lithium-polymer (Lipo) batteries have become very popular in modern electronics due to their thin profile and high gravimetric energy. Two Lipo cells, from Varta Microbatteries, with a capacity of 1.3Ah each are used as the main secondary battery in the YuSend-1 spacecraft. They are 6.22cm long, with a width of 3.5cm and a height of 0.52cm. They have mass of 24g and are capable of providing 4.88Wh each. The batteries are currently undergoing series of tests (see Table 2) to characterize the cell for space applications.

High efficiency solar cells such as the XTJ solar cells from Spectrolab, with an efficiency of 29.9%, have been identified for our mission. In the power distribution module (PDM) design, two distinct models were compared: Direct Energy Transfer (DET) and Peak-power Transfer (PPT) methods. It was determined that the PPT method is the ideal option for the purpose of a LEO mission since there are many eclipses per orbit. These eclipses will cause large performance shifts of the solar array assembly due to the frequently varying temperature. The PPT will be able to exploit this characteristic of the arrays and maximize power production.

Table 2. Lithium polymer battery tests

Tests	Description
Self Discharge	Cell is discharged then charged and stored (open circuit) over 48 hours. It is then discharged and measured to examine how much power was lost while being stored.
Charge/Discharge Rates	Three different cells are charged and discharged using the following rates: C, C/5, and C/10, in order to determine at which rate the capacity loss and resistance is minimized.
Temperature	The capacity and internal resistance of the battery is measured as the cell is being cycled at: -10, 0 and 40 °C.
Depth of Discharge (DoD):	Two cells are cycled at C/5 to a DoD of 30% and 80% in order to examine the effects of deep discharging on the life of the battery.
Vacuum Test	Cells are cycled once and have their capacity checked before being placed in the thermal vacuum chamber. They are then cycled at different rates and to different DoD in the reduced pressure environment, in order to determine the effects a vacuum on the capacity of the battery over time.

1.2.2 Attitude Control Components

Fig. 3. PL-A633 camera, used in star tracker development

The need for low-cost, high accuracy attitude and orbit control system (AOCS) components has also grown exponentially in the past decade. With MEMS and nanotechnologies continuously pushing the envelope of space engineering, the tools necessary for small and accurate attitude control are now available. In response to the current trend for miniaturization in space, the development of AOCS components suitable for nanosatellite missions has been of great interest. In addition to innovative component design, YuSend-1 will contain robust attitude determination and control algorithms. Development of these algorithms, such as the improving of sub-pixel interpolation for centroiding in star cameras, has already begun for YuSend-1. Fig. 3 to Fig. 5 represent some of the current tools for AOCS development.

1.2.3 Nano-Wheels

A miniature reaction wheel suitable for CubeSat-style satellites is currently being developed by the YuSend team. Such nano-wheels are designed to provide a nominal torque of less than 5 mNm, resulting in a momentum of about 40 mNm-sec. The target power consumption (in steady state) is 0.5W while operating at 5V. The goal for the wheel's mass is 200 g. Currently there are several university-based satellite missions testing this technology, including the University of Toronto's CanX-2. Currently, there is no common production means for these wheels, so individual wheels must be ordered specially or produced in-house. The wheel works in conjunction with magnetorquer coils to provide the required pointing accuracy and stability.

1.2.4 Magnetorquers

The magnetorquers (magnetic torque coils) are designed to be YuSend-1's main set of actuators. They will provide momentum dumping for the nano-wheel, and orientation-locking for the micro-thruster firings. There are three of these, aligned with the spacecraft's x, y and z-axis. The dipole created by passing current through the coils will create a torque aligning the dipole with the local geomagnetic field.

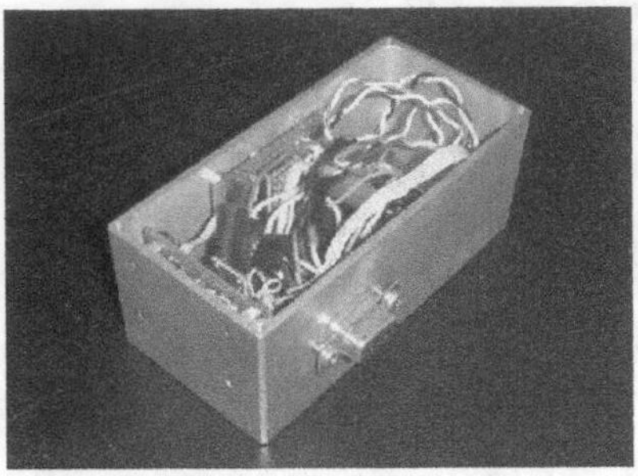

Fig. 4. Three-axis rate sensor suite

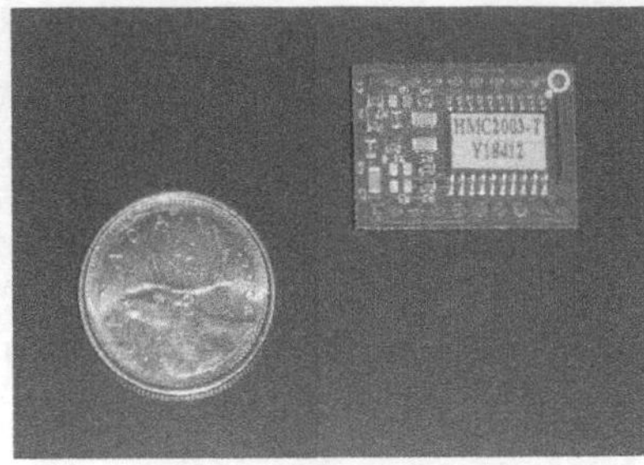

Fig. 5. HMC2003 flight-prototype magntometer to be used in YuSend-1

YuSend-1 will have PCB-inlayed magnetorquers. The benefits of these over the traditional wrapped coils are: 1) Certainty in the design specifications 2) Reproducibility 3) Simpler mounting of the boards for assembly of the satellite and 4) Vibrational robustness. A B-dot control will implemented to control the magnetorquers during satellite detumbling. When the nano-wheel is active, all actuators will be controlled via a PID controller. The ACS simulation is under development in Matlab and will be extended to hardware-in-the-loop test-bed.

1.2.5 Microthrusters

State-of-the-art micro-thrusters, suitable for nanosatellite missions, have been surveyed. The micro-propulsion system considered for YuSend-1 is a micro pulsed plasma thruster (μPPT). It consists of two electrodes (anode and cathode), a trigger device, a capacitor, a propellant (Teflon), and other electronics. It works by initially building up a large charge in the capacitor, which is then discharged across the electrodes. This high energy discharge ablates the Teflon propellant bar which is located between the electrodes resulting in ionized atoms/molecules. These ionized particles are accelerated via the Lorenz force which is the interaction between charged particles and an electromagnetic field.

One of the reasons that a μPPT is very suitable for our application is that its structural simplicity lends itself to miniaturization. It has no moving parts such as valves which reduces complexity and thus reliability. Other advantages include a high specific impulse, low power consumption, and the space proven aspect.

On the YuSend-1 mission, two μPPTs, which are positioned on the opposite face of the spacecraft from the camera, is planned. These two thrusters will be used for linear and rotational movement. Magnetorquers will bring the spacecraft to the correct orientation and both thrusters firing simultaneously will provide the push in that direction. Thrusters firing individually will provide rotational movement. This will meet the attitude control and orbit change demonstration objectives.

1.2.6 Autonomous Mission Planning

The technology that brings the above components and algorithms together is the semi-autonomous control strategy. In many space missions, there is heavy reliance on a schedule of events requiring ground operator inputs. In missions with stringent power and communication budget, such pre-planned missions often result in loss of critical observation time. A new approach is being investigated, called autonomous mission planning, where the system monitors the health of the components to make intelligent command decisions from the mission scenario. The ground operator issues a simple, high-level command and the spacecraft automatically generates a string of mission specific commands. In cases of a component failure or unforeseen events, the planner updates the mission scenario to optimize the performance and utilize the remaining functionality of the spacecraft. Through the YuSend demonstration mission, we are developing an autonomous nanosatellite that can not only maximize the observation time (via camera demonstration) but also perform attitude and orbit adjustment (via thruster demonstration) autonomously in preparation for autonomous formation flying and stereo imaging missions.

1.3 Facilities at York

1.3.1 Vibration Testing

The vibration test facility consists of a Dynamic Solutions DS-3300/12-15 electrodynamic shaker capable of producing more than 10 kN of force over the frequency range of 10 – 3000 Hz. The shaker is housed within a custom-built, physically isolated and soundproof room. The shaker provides excitation in one axis. Other axes are tested by means of a test fixture that provides three orthogonal mounting faces. Additionally, the system can deliver shock loads exceeding 100g. The system instrumentation includes four accelerometer channels operated via a computer and control electronics. The software can perform sine sweep, random and classical shock tests.

1.3.2 Thermal Vacuum Testin

The thermal vacuum chamber provides a means to test the spacecraft and instrumentation under the environmental conditions experienced after launch. The pumping system is typically able to provide an ultimate pressure below 10-6 torr. A horizontal 1.5m diameter chamber has an access door for the installation of equipment. The system includes a 2m platen that can roll partially out of the chamber for component loading and assembly. The custom built system can cycle temperatures between +140 °C and -140°C in order to induce thermal cycle loading analogous to that experienced by space hardware on Mars. A chamber shroud with liquid nitrogen circulation is included to provide a means of simulating the radiative background of space. Customized characterization experiments simulating planetary atmospheres and other pressure environments can be performed according to a programmable temperature cycle.

1.3.3 Assembly and Integration

In addition to the environmental testing facilities, the satellite assembly area is co-located with the space instrument integration and test facility. The facility includes 100,000-class and 10,000-class clean rooms, electronics shop, fully equipped machine shop and computer laboratories with software tools such as ProE, MATLAB, STK, and LabView.

1.3.4 Ground Station

As mentioned earlier, our group is assembling a ground station compatible with the GENSO ground station network. This ground station hardware consists of commercially available equipment and will operate in the amateur 2-m and 70-cm (VHF/UHF) bands. Faculty and students have recently been qualified as amateur radio operators. In order to operate the station, several control programs were also acquired and installed on the operations computer including Uni-TRAC 2003, Nova and Satellite Tool Kit (STK).

1.4 Final Remarks

The YuSend program builds on the existing space science and engineering programs at York University. These programs have a rich history, as York has been a home to the Centre for Research in Earth and Space Sciences (CRESS) since the 1970s. Recently, space engineers and scientists from CRESS delivered meteorological instrumentation for the Phoenix Mars Lander mission that landed on Mars. This successful collaboration with other universities and NASA is providing data on Martian atmospheric chemistry, among other research.

York University prides itself on its diversified and driven student body. The York engineering program is composed of three specialist streams, one being Space Engineering. This strong emphasis on a solid space engineering core is reflected in the research being conducted by the many space professors, graduate and undergraduates through both professional and student projects. The York space engineering students recently competed as the only Canadian entry in the University Rover Challenge, an international competition organized by the Mars Society. The York Rover team placed third in the competition, proving our teamwork and engineering skills. See [2] for more details. The YuSend team has been also recently chosen for the SSETI SWARM mission to provide guidance in the area of space environmental effects. For details on this student-led Cubesat mission, see [3].

The authors would like to thank Prof. Brendan Quine and Dr. Caroline Roberts for their input on the description of the facilities. We also would like to acknowledge the following students for their contribution to the paper: Fem Gandhi, Piratheepan Jeyakumar and Mark Post.

References

[1] Baty, R.S. 2003, 'Space Propulsion', Air Force Rocket Propulsion Laboratory, [Online] Available at: http://www.airpower.maxwell.af.mil/airchronicles/aureview/1973/nov-dec/baty.html

[2] http://www.marssociety.org/portal/Members/schnarff/URC2008Results/ - Accessed August 2008.

[3] http://www.sseti.net/ - Accessed August 2008.

[4] Klofas, B., Anderson, J., "A Survey of CubeSat Communications Systems", NSF Cubesat Developers Workshop, April 2008, accessed at http://atl.calpoly.edu/~bklofas/Presentations/DevelopersWorkshop2008/CommSurvey-Bryan_Klofas.pdf, September 2008.

A Dynamic Bridge for Data Sharing on e-Science Grid Implementing Web 2.0 Service

Im Y. Jung and Heon Y. Yeom

School of CSE, Seoul Nat'l Univ., San 56-1, Shinlim-Dong, Kwanak-Gu, 151-742, Seoul, South Korea, e-mail: iyjung@dcslab.snu.ac.kr, yeom@snu.ac.kr

Abstract This paper proposes a dynamic bridge for e-Science Grid, implementing Web 2.0 service in order to share experimental data effectively.An e-Science Grid has been established as a cyber laboratory for the users with a special research purpose on science. As an open space, e-Science Grid is expected to stimulate the collaborative researches and the cross domain ones. These research trends need a more efficient and convenient data service satisfying the science researchers. A dynamic bridge designed based on HVEM DataGrid, satisfies the users' requirements for the data sharing on e-Science Grid effectively. It supports a data tagging service in order for HVEM DataGrid to be utilized more extensively without any modification of the existing Grid architecture or services. Moreover, it can be adopted and deleted easily without any effect to the legacy Grid. With the legacy interface to access data in e-Science Grid, the data tags endow the Grid with the flexibility for data access. This paper evaluates the usefulness of the dynamic bridge by analyzing its overhead and performance.

Keywords: e-Science Grid, science data sharing, Web 2.0 service, HVEM DataGrid, a dynamic bridge

1 Introduction

E-Science Grid has been established as a cyber laboratory for the users with a special research purpose on science. It was designed as an optimized system considering the research custom and the convenience of its Virtual Organization (VO) members. For example, HVEM DataGrid [2] was specialized for the data

DOI 10.1007/978-1-4419-1719-5_8,

management of the biological research. It provides a search service based on the data model and the search methods which are well known to biologists. CCDB [3] is another example for the databank for biologists. Although the data increases fast and its volume gets large accordingly in e-Science Grid, if the data services stick to a particular search mechanism which considers the search pattern of the researchers in one science domain for example, they would not satisfy the researchers studying other sciences. The researchers would suffer a difficulty in using search keywords unfamiliar and an overhead to reach the information they want by several search steps for cross domain research. As an open space, e-Science Grid is expected to stimulate the collaborative researches and the cross domain ones. These research trends need a more efficient and convenient data service satisfying the researchers.

As the user-centric services are watched with deep concern and developed, the service developers have a difficulty in the complex service adoption and the service standard establishment. Web 2.0 philosophy is welcomed with the expectation of solving the problems. Prominent examples are delicious, Bibsonomy, and Connotea. They illustrate the following concepts of Web 2.0 services [5][6]; tagging, searching and discovery by tags, network building, and multiple user interfaces. E-Science Grid can provide the enhanced services by importing web 2.0 philosophy. That is, the tagging service can compensate the semantic loss in the process of digitization and formalization of the experimental data in e-Science Grid. And, the data search by tag can complement the search service provided by e-Science Grid. There is a difficulty for the researchers to communicate and understand each other when their knowledge backgrounds are different in the collaborative research through e-Science Grid. By making an indirect channel to access to the objects in e-Science Grid, the tagging service can mitigates the difficulty. A network can be established among the researchers who have a common research interest. But, due to its expensive resources and invaluable data, e-Science Grid is different from WWW which is open to anyone. Therefore, a new community network or a new data service should be considered in the restricted open space of e-Science Grid.

This paper proposes a dynamic bridge for e-Science Grid in order to share science data effectively. It supports a data tagging service in order for HVEM DataGrid to be utilized more extensively. With the legacy interface to access data in e-Science DataGrid, it endows the Grid with the flexibility for data access. Because the data tags are created by the researchers as needed, their volume can grow rapidly. The data search using the tags can be slower than that through the existing interface of HVEM DataGrid. But, the former can compensate the data service provided by HVEM DataGrid with the tags added actively. Therefore, if the performance of the bridge is not much less than the legacy interface, it is meaningful to introduce the dynamic bridge to e-Science Grid. The positive effects which are expected from the dynamic bridge are as follows. First, the dynamic bridge in this paper can endow a freedom to the researchers in e-Science environment as in the offline laboratory by providing them with a private space of data tagging to supplement their researches. Second, it maximizes the advantage of collaborative research through e-Science environment. Due to the syntax-free format of data tag, collaborative tagging systems have a low barrier to promote researchers' participation. The free annotations during experimental process compensate the formalized data stored in e-Science Grid. And, the additional information from data tag helps the researches through e-Science environment. The cyber laboratory and cyber experimental process can be activated than now though the data tagging service.

The rest of this paper is organized as follows. Section 2 describes the previous works on web 2.0 services, tagging service and the technologies related. Section 3.1 describes a dynamic bridge for an enhanced data service on e-Science Grid. Section 4 demonstrates the soundness of the proposed scheme by analyzing its performance and overhead. Conclusion and future works are presented in Section 5.

2 Related Works

One example to apply Web 2.0 technology to research domain is MSI-CIEC [8]. It provides a means to create communities of like-minded faculty and researchers, particularly at minority serving institutions. MSI-CIEC focuses on the architecture for the researchers to reach each other easily by tagging service. As an open system, it allows a collaborative tagging. But, the tagging system to support a collaborative research on e-Science Grid should allow a restricted tagging service because the authorization for the data in e-Science Grid is different according to the Grid users basically.

The vector model and the graph model are well known as the tag management models. The vector model [16] is useful in that the researchers and the data tags to be used are pre-defined. We can know the frequency to use a tag easily with the vector model. On the other hand, the graph model [9] has a representative feature of scalability. The tag graph represents a relationship among the users as well as the tag information for the objects. The tags in e-Science Grid are different from the ones which are in WWW. The latter are related to the users' tastes proven by reference statistics. But, the former are deeply related to the knowledge background, the research habit and the research interest of the users.

As more users participate in tagging, so the tag space is bigger. For the large tag space, a fast and efficient search method is studied. To apply data clustering is one example. Several algorithms are proposed. For the vector model, hierarchical clustering [10], k-means clustering [11], and deterministic annealing algorithm [12] are suggested. For the graph model, FolkRank [13] and graph-based clustering algorithm [14][15] are proposed. As a derivative of PageRank in Google, FolkRank clusters the tags by ranking the graph component such as tag, user, and resource. The graph-based clustering analyzes the links in the tag graph and clusters the tags. For most tag graphs, people use the tag graph analysis for clustering. However, e-Science Grid has its own objective to provide a cyber research environment for scientists. And, because the objects in e-Science Grid come from the research process, the tags for the objects may also related to the science research. That is, the tags would largely depend on the knowledge background and the research interest of the user to tag. Therefore, in e-Science Grid, we can expect a better data service to apply them to tag clustering as a heuristic before to analyze the tag graph.

On the other hand, the tags should be managed with the objects related. One study proposes an event-based approach to manage the consistency of data and the tags related [7]. The collaborative tagging can cause the inconsistency problem. To prevent the inconsistency, the approach classifies the events which are generated when there are the changes in the objects as a major event and a minor event. The former notifies that an object is created or deleted. The latter does that an object is updated. Until a major event happens, minor events are delayed to be applied. It is somewhat not free to tag the objects in e-Science because there are the access restraints for the objects in e-Science Grid. And, the changes of the objects are not frequent compared with the objects in WWW. And, because the tags function as the memos in the research process, it would be desirable to sublate the update or the deletion by the other users.

3 A Dynamic Bridge for efficient sharing of e-Science resources

3.1 Architecture and Protocol

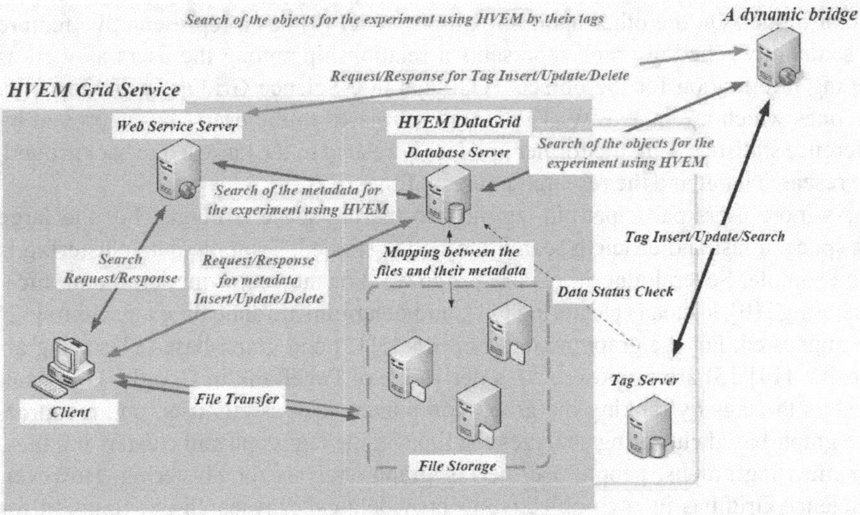

Fig. 1. Architecture of dynamic bridge

As shown in fig. 1, the dynamic bridge support the tagging service in e-Science Grid. Without belonging to the legacy e-Science Grid, it provides a tagging service in addition to the existing data service in the e-Science Grid. That is, users can tag the objects privately through the dynamic bridge and search the objects by the tags. As an additional information, the tag can be a communication channel for the users with the same knowledge background and the same research interest in e-Science Grid. The dynamic bridge is significant structurally as a way to provide additional data service in need without any request for the modification of the legacy e-Science Grid.

The tagging service through the dynamic bridge has the following mechanism. First, it takes the tag for an object in HVEM Grid. Because the users have their own accessibility to the objects in HVEM Grid [2], the tag for an object also can be inserted or updated by the user who has the authorization to the object. And, the users get the restricted search results by tag according to their accessibility. During the data search though the legacy interface of HVEM DataGrid, when the search web service takes the tag insert request, the web service transfers the object identity, the tag to be inserted, and the user identity to the dynamic bridge. The information transferred is stored in the tag server by the dynamic bridge. The tag server checks the status of the objects to be tagged and the users periodically. In the period between status check, there are the changes on the objects or the users in HVEM Grid, they are reflected to the tag server. When the objects to be tagged are deleted in HVEM Grid, it is needless for the tag server to keep the tags related. But, when the users are deleted, the tags they inserted are not deleted. The search by tag is initiated by sending the tag to be used and the user identity to the dynamic bridge. Then, the objects related to the tag are searched in the tag server. When there is the object identity related, the information for the object is retrieved in HVEM Grid. But, when the user to search the object has no accessibility to it, he can not get the search result for the object.

3.2 Data Tagging Service

3.2.1 The objects for Tagging Service

All the objects in e-Science Grid can be tagged. Fig. 2 shows the objects to be tagged in HVEM DataGrid. The objects in the schema of HVEM DataGrid include the experimental data using HVEM and the metadata related.

3.2.2 A new graph model for Data Tagging

It is difficult to understand the tendency of the tags related to the researchers when the research groups participating in the collaborative researches are various and not fixed in e-Science Grid. As a private memo during research process, in order to let the tag contribute to enhancing the e-Science environment which can provide an user-centric data service, it would be better to unlimit the tag space. Therefore, this paper propose a new graph model considering the characteristic of e-Science Grid.

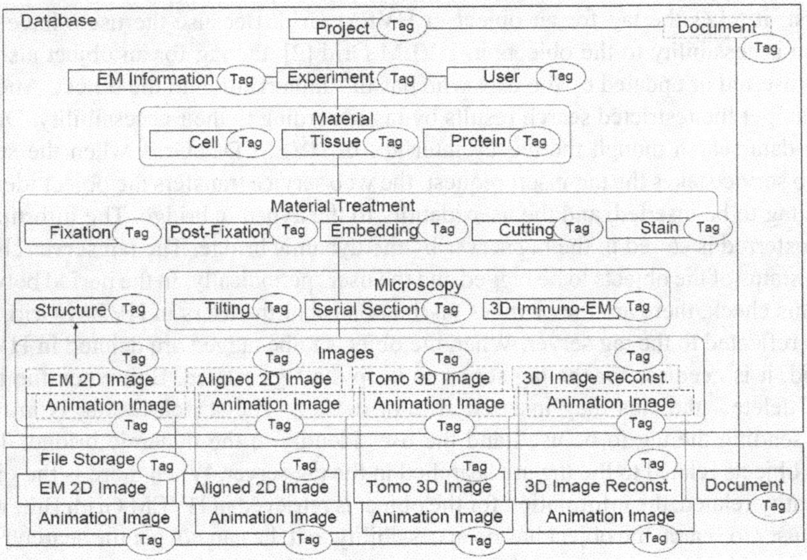

Fig. 2. The objects to be tagged in HVEM DataGrid

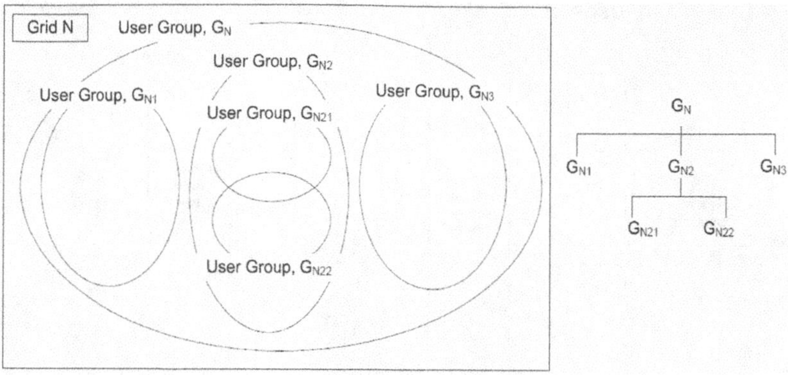

Fig. 3. User Clustering according to research domain

The data in e-Science Grid is stored and managed, optimized with its schema. But, the tags are inserted by the users without any form or schema, it is not easy to manage them. Even in the case that the increasing rate for the objects is not high, that for the tags can be. The search by the tags can take a long time. To lessen the search overhead, this paper uses a tag clustering according to the users to tag.

- User Clustering

As an e-Science Grid, HVEM Grid controls the access to its resources by its users' roles [2]. And, in order to use the Grid resources, the users should belong to the Grid in advance. The users participating in the collaborative researches can be be clustered according to their knowledge background and research interests because e-Science Grid is basically established with its own objective, to support special science research. And, the tags in e-Science Grid can be categorized according to the cluster of the users to tag because, as well as the objects in e-Science Grid, they would be depend on the users. Therefore, this paper groups the tags and manages the tag clusters hierarchically according to the users to tag. Because the user information is kept when a user registers in the HVEM Grid, his research interest and knowledge background can be clustered hierarchically as shown in fig. 3. The tags are clustered as the same with the users' information.

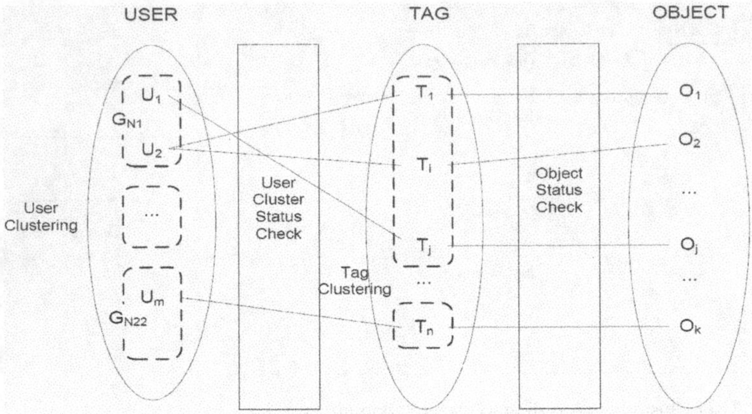

Fig. 4. a new graph model

- A new graph model

The information saved in the tag server is (user identity, tag, object identity, user group identity). In fig. 4, one example is ($U1$, Tj, Oj, $GN1$). For the efficient search by user clustering, the user group hierarchy is referenced as shown in the right side of fig. 3. Therefore, the search by tag is done according to the group of the users to tag step by step.

Because the tags in HVEM Grid are defined as a private memo in the research process, it is not allowed for other users to update the tags. But, users can use the search by the tags which are created by other users.

4 Evaluation

4.1 Performance of tag management

It is assumed that the user clustering is done with the user information in e-Science Grid in advance and the user group information is stored in both the DB in HVEM DataGrid and the tag server.

Then, the search by tag is executed according to the following steps. First, the dynamic bridge takes the user identity who requests the search and the tag to be used as search keyword. Second, the dynamic bridge search the objects related to the tag in the tag server. Third, it sends the objects searched in HVEM DataGrid, which the user can access.

The tag insert by the dynamic bridge is done according to the following steps. First, the dynamic bridge takes the object identity which is to be tagged, the tag, the user identity who is to tag. Second, it inserts the information with the information of the user cluster related, to the tag server.

The sequences are a little different with those of the legacy data service in HVEM DataGrid [2]. Those are the user clustering and the step 2 in the search process and the tag insert process. But, the step 2 in both processes is a necessary step when the tag server is established separated from the storages in DataGrid. The user clustering is an unique process in this paper.

4.1.1 Tag Clustering Effect

We can estimate search latency according to tag increase in order to know the effect of the tag clustering. We let the number of tags be n. And, they are assumed to be clustered to a groups. Then, the search efficiency will be highest when all the users participate in tagging and the tags belong to a groups evenly. In this case, O(freqna) can be the search efficiency. When only one user tags, the worst efficiency would be O(n). That is, the search efficiency would depend on the users activity for tagging and the user clustering. When the user clustering is adopted in the tagging service in e-Science Grid targeting the collaborative researches, the search efficiency would be sought first of all. Because the e-Science Grid is a domain with a clear objective of science research, the characteristics of the users can be defined clearly and classified easily. The tags are affected by the users' characteristics because they are created by the users. The clustering can lessen the search overhead according to the tag increase. When a is small or only some users tag, we may consider the clustering methods provided by the previous works [13][14][15] as secondary methods. But, these secondary methods cause an overhead, which does not overcome performance, when the tags are not many. And, the clusterings only considering the tag characteristics are quite within the realms of possibility to be imperfect semantically. Therefore, after the user clustering is applied, it would be effective to consider the tag clustering as a secondary method in e-Science Grid.

4.1.2 Overhead Analysis for the dynamic bridge

- User Clustering Cost

The user clustering in e-Science Grid is easier than that in WWW because the users in e-Science Grid should be registered with his information. The user information for knowledge background, research interest and the research projects related are included.

- The Cost for Data Consistency according to Tag Increase

Because the changes on the objects and the users in e-Science Grid, are rare compared with WWW, it is enough for the tag server to check the status of the objects related to their tags and the users periodically. In the research process, it is not often for the research products to be deleted or to be updated because all the objects are important in the research process. Even in the update, the object is not substituted by a new object; the new object is stored additionally as another data. The user clusters can be changed. But, it is not common because the users' knowledge background can not be changed. A new background and a new research interest may be added to the user information. When there is a change in the user clustering, the change is applied to the tag server by the periodic status check. When a user is deleted in e-Science Grid, the tags are maintained. But, the tags can not be modified any more. The cost to maintain the consistency between the objects and their tags would not cause to drop the data service quality because the period for status check can be adapted for the tag server and only the changes between the check points are inspected. In the worst case, the search efficiency would drop temporarily when there is a problem in the data consistency. But, this does not cause any disaster in the data system.

Therefore, the dynamic bridge ensures a relative low search latency and management cost insensitive to the increasing rate of the data tags.

5 Conclusion and Future Works

This paper proposes a dynamic bridge, which provides a private data tagging for e-Science Grid as an additional data service, and analyzes its usefulness. The dynamic bridge shows the following features. The dynamic bridge provides a dynamicity of an easy installation and deletion to the existing e-Science Grid with an impact for its entire structure as less as possible. It is undesirable if e-Science Grid should be redesigned for its overall structure when a new paradigm or functionality is added. Therefore, the bridge has a desirable feature in order to be applicable to e-Science Grid. The dynamic bridge enables a user centric data search service by supplementing a function to manage the personalized data tags in the e-Science DataGrid. By the private tagging service, the users can stand by their own research habits in the offline laboratory even in the cyber-laboratory. This is expected to cause a positive effect to boost creative researches in their familiar environment. Moreover, the dynamic bridge provides a consistent management of the data tags considering the data status in e-Science Grid.

On the other hand, even though the data tags mean additional information for the objects in e-Science Grid, they should not be open to anyone. As a private memo, the tags should be open according to their own policy which may be somewhat different from the data in e-Science Grid. The policy for management and security can be another research issue.

References

1. A. M. Akito MONDEN and C. THOMBORSON. Tamper-resistant software system based on a finite state machine. IEICE transactions on fundamentals of electronics, communications and computer science, 88(1):112–122, 2005.
2. Im Young Jung, In Soon Cho, Heon Y. Yeom, Hee S. Kweon and Jysoo Lee. HVEM DataGrid: Implementation of a Biologic Data Management System for Experiments with High Voltage Electron Microscope. Distributed, High-Performance and Grid Computing in Computational Biology (GCCB 2006),Jan. 2007.
3. http://ccdb.uscd.edu/CCDB/
4. Seung-Jin Kwak and Jeong-Taek Kim. A Study on the Development of High Voltage Electron Microscope Metadata Model for Efficient Management and Sharing. Journal of Korean library and information science society, 38(3):117–138, 2007.
5. Geoffrey C. Fox et al.. Web 2.0 for Grids and e-Science. Instrumenting the Grid 2nd International Workshop on Distributed Cooperative Laboratories(INGRID 2007), ITALY, April, 2007.
6. Geoffrey C. Fox et al.. Web 2.0 for E-Science Environments. 3rd International Conference on Semantics, Knowledge and Grid(SKG2007), China, October, 2007.
7. Ahmet Fatih Mustacoglu, Ahmet E. Topcu Aurel Cami, Geoffrey Fox. A Novel Event-Based Consistency Model for Supporting Collaborative Cyberinfrastructure Based Scientific Research. Proceedings of The 2007 International Symposium on Collaborative Technologies and Systems (CTS 2007), 2007.
8. Marlon E. Pierce, Geoffrey C. Fox, Joshua Rosen, Siddharth Maini, and Jong Y. Choi. Social networking for scientists using tagging and shared bookmarks: a Web 2.0 application. International Symposium on Collaborative Technologies and Systems (CTS 2008), 2008
9. H. Halpin, V. Robu, and H. Shepherd. The Complex Dynamics of Collaborative Tagging. In Proceedings of the 16th international Conference on World Wide Web(WWW'07), ACM, New York, 211–220, 2007.
10. Y. Zhao, G. Karypis and U. Fayyad. Hierarchical Clustering Algorithms for Document Datasets. Data Mining and Knowledge Discovery, 10:141–168, 2005.
11. C. Ding and X. He. K-means clustering via principal component analysis. ACM International Conference Proceeding Series, 2004.
12. K. Rose. Deterministic Annealing for Clustering, Compression, Classification, Regression and Related Optimization Problems. Proc. IEEE, 86:2210–2239, 1998.
13. A. Hotho, R. Jaschke, C. Schmitz and G. Stumme. Information retrieval in folksonomies: Search and ranking. The Semantic Web: Research and Applications, 4011:411–426, 2006.
14. G. Karypis, E.H.Han and V. Kumar. Chameleon: hierarchical clustering using dynamic modeling. Computer, 32:68–75, 1999.
15. E. Hartuv, and R. Shamir. A clustering algorithm based on graph connectivity. Information Processing Letters, 76:175–181, 2000.
16. G. Salton, A. Wong, C.S. Yang. A vector space model for automatic indexing. Commun. ACM, 18(11):613–620, 1975.

A Grid Middleware Framework Support for a Workflow Model Based on Virtualized Resources

Jinbock Lee, Sangkeon Lee and Jaeyoung Choi

Department of Computing, Soongsil University, Seoul, Korea
{jeinbi, seventy9, choi}@ssu.ac.kr

Abstract Nowadays, the virtualization technologies are widely used to overcome the difficulty of managing Grid computing infrastructures. The virtual account and the virtual workspace are very optimistic to allocate Grid resources to specific user, but they lacks of capability of interaction between portal services and virtualized resources which required by Grid portal. The virtual application is fitted to wrap simple application as a Grid portal service, but integrating some applications to compose larger application service is difficult. In this paper, we present a Grid middleware framework which supports for a workflow model based on virtualized resources. Meta Services in the framework exposes workflow as a portal service and service call is converted different workflow according to parameter and workflow generated by the Meta Services is scheduled in a virtual cluster which configured by this framework. Because of virtual application service can be composed of workflow and service interface wraps the workflow providing a complex portal services composed by small application could effectively integrated to Grid portal and scheduled in virtual computing resources.

1 Introduction

e-Science environments have large scale and heavy data throughput. These environments need a lot of applications, and it consists of workflows. When workflows are submitted and executed, the workflows can require various environments such as different O/S, special H/W, memory capacity or several external devices. To support these environments effectively, new mechanism is needed in e-Science and Grid environments.

Nowadays, the virtualization technologies are widely used to overcome the difficulty of managing Grid computing infrastructures. As the virtualization technology is integrated with a Grid environment, the computing system provides

O.-H. Byeon et al. (eds.), *Future Application and Middleware Technology on e-Science*,
DOI 10.1007/978-1-4419-1719-5_9, © Springer Science+Business Media, LLC 2010

with more various and extended environments. For example, physical resource can be abstracted and separated to virtualized resources, such as CPU, memory, storage and NIC. These virtualized resources can be re-configured dynamically as the system requires more resource capacities.

Virtualization technologies are widely used to overcome difficulty of managing heterogeneous and large scale computing resources in the Grid Computing. Among them, the virtual workspace which integrates virtual machines into a virtual cluster and which provides the cluster to user with isolation to other user is the most spotlighted recently. Using the virtual accounts and the virtual workspaces is the most popular approach to integrate virtualization technology to Grid environment. The virtual account and the virtual workspace are very optimistic to allocate Grid resources to specific user, but they lacks of capability of interaction between portal services and virtualized resources which required by Grid portal. But, in the Grid based e-Science portal, application is shared among users as a common portal services and integrating the services into virtual computing resources is also important.

The InVIGO approach proposed by the ACIS lab in university of Florida uses the virtual application concept that wraps legacy application with application interface generated by rule and virtualized computing environments. The virtual application could provide a legacy application as a "virtual" application which has a various parameter format that each user in portal requires. A virtual application concept which wraps a physical application as a service is applied to Grid frameworks to integrate portal services to virtualized Grid resources. The virtual application is fitted to wrap simple application as a Grid portal service, but integrating some applications to compose larger application service is difficult. Due to lack of workflow managements in the virtual application in the InVIGO, the virtual application cannot be applied to bio informatics portal where workflow management is key feature. To handle these requirements of management of virtual computing resources mainly virtual machines, workflow management, integrating application and workflow into portal service, we defined a middleware framework called MSF (Meta Services Framework).

MSF provides a middle-ware framework which provides essential functionalities to construct a Grid portal especially BT Grid portal. The functionalities provides by the MSF are workflow composition, integration of the workflow as a portal services, distribution of workflow task on grid resources, managing grid resources as a virtual cluster and virtual application management using software streaming technology. Meta Services concept of the MSF virtualizes a workflow which composed of legacy applications and DAG containing control path and data path among the applications instead of virtualizes a legacy application. After a meta service called by user with a set of service parameters, it analyzed and instantiated as a workflow by meta service engine and later the workflow scheduled on a virtual cluster by the workflow engine. After workflow is scheduled, subtasks of the workflow executed on work nodes constructed by virtual machines. When a subtask requires an application not installed on the virtual machine, binary part of the application is streamed from server and the application executed.

2 System Architecture

The overall architecture of the MSF is shown in the figure 1. Whole system consists of triple layers - worknode layer, workflow layer and portal service layer. The worknode layer on the bottom consists of virtual machine, virtual software and EM module. Virtual machine is used to configure a work node independent to physical machine configuration. Virtual software is used to remove overhead of managing binary and configuration of the software form each virtual machines. And the EM executes workflow tasks scheduled by above layer.

The workflow layer on the middle of the architecture manages virtual clusters and scheduling workflow on the virtual cluster. RM module in the layers allocates and releases virtual machines to physical nodes using virtual machine monitors in each node. After virtual machine is created, EM module in the VM connects to the RM which requested creation of virtual machine and notify now execution of workflow task is ready. When EM notifies more subtask could be executed, RM distributes workflow task to the RM.

The portal service layer in the top of the architecture, service request from users converted to workflow to be executed by SM. SM process user's service requests, make a instance of workflow, overriding attributes of workflow and subtasks using Meta Services and issues a workflow execution requests to RM. Meta Services contains information of how to handle a service and parameter request and instantiating a workflow instance.

On all of layers, authentication is processed by AM and ontology management is performed by OM. When user logins to the portal, grid proxy certificates generated and stored to AM. If user authentication or grid proxy certificates are required, modules in MSF connect to AM and check authentication or retrieve the proxy certification. OM manages description of service, flow, task and virtual machine configuration in XML form and provides the description when other components requested the description. Currently, aPod server is not integrated to MSF architecture, so virtual software is separately managed by aPod server.

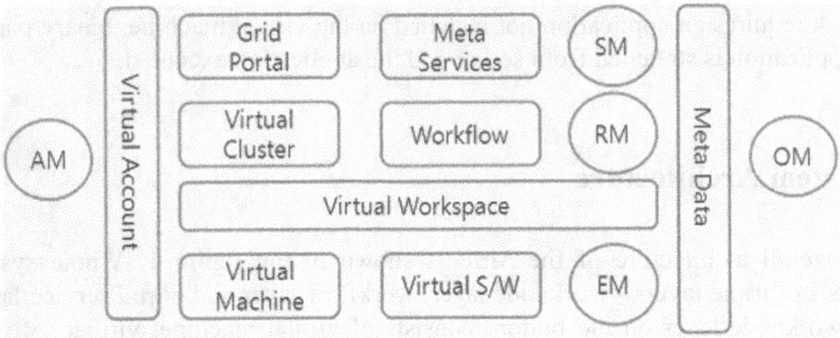

Fig. 1. System Architecture of MSF.

3 Management of Virtual Cluster

In MSF architecture, RM constructs a virtual cluster using VMM installed on physical worknodes. Administrator could easily control resources of a virtual cluster by creating and releasing virtual machine. When a VM is created, RM allocates virtual machine id, ip address, hostname and virtual MAC address for VM. After the allocation, configuration file is generated and VM is started by VMM. After linux operating system in the VM booted up, a shell script configures and boots up the globus toolkit and EM.

A worknode of MSF is constructed as figure 2. VMWare is installed on every physical machine as a VMM. Linux operating system is installed on virtual machine image as a Guest OS. Globus toolkit is used to construct basic Grid middleware services such as a program execution, file transfer and etc. While executing a software aPod client download and cache parts of software binary from server as it needed. That is a concept of software streaming. Operating system could recognize streamed part of software as a full part of software through virtual file system. To implement the virtual file system layer, aPod software streaming client uses FUSE file system bundled on the Linux system.

On the start time, EM determines number of virtual processors from the virtual machine configuration and decides that how many subtasks can be executed. The number of subtasks is a multiple of the number of virtual processors and can be configured. After setup is finished, EM reports its status to RM and RM updates resource information of virtual cluster.

When administrator requested to release a virtual machine, EM hosted by the virtual machine is marked and no All of more subtask allocated to the EM. And allocated subtask is completed, EM notifies subtask completion to RM and RM shut down the virtual machine. The shutdown of virtual machine is also canceled by the administrator. After the virtual machine is shut downed, hostname, ip address and etc allocated by the RM returned and can be used to allocation of new virtual machine.

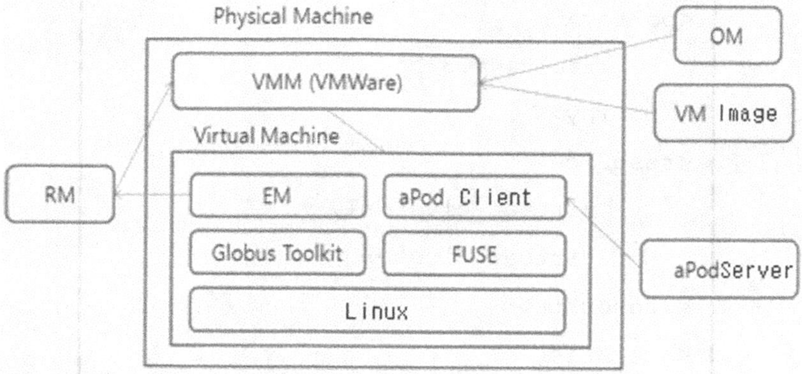

Fig. 2. Construction of a Worknode in MSF

4 Meta Services

Meta Services defines a service interface, policy, resource and modification of workflow attribute according to service parameter. By using the Meta Services, a workflow could be utilized as multiple type of service and satisfy man users without modifying the workflow. Example of a meta service is shown in figure 3. First line defines service name and parameter list. In the policy section service policy is defined such as number of fault tolerable while executing workflows. In the resource section list of virtual cluster that can be used for these service. Workflow engine select one of virtual cluster in the list while scheduling workflows. In the execution section workflow description imported, define workflow instance and instance name and exchange value of workflow attributes with service parameter passed to the meta service.

```
MetaService M2 (p1)
<policy>
      fault <= 3
</policy>
<resource>
      virtual_cluster1,
      virtual_cluster3
</resource>
<execution>
      import Workflow HG2C as whg2c;
      whg2c.t1.protein = p1;
</execution>
```

Fig. 3. Example of a Meta Service

5 Related Researches

A comparison of MSF to other researches related resource virtualization in Grid computing is shown in fig. 4. Virtual account concept is resides in Globus toolkit and implemented as GSI using a extend X.509 certificates and maps local system account with a global user id. The global user id defined in the Globus is a virtual account and mapped to real system id and valid in limited time defined by system user.

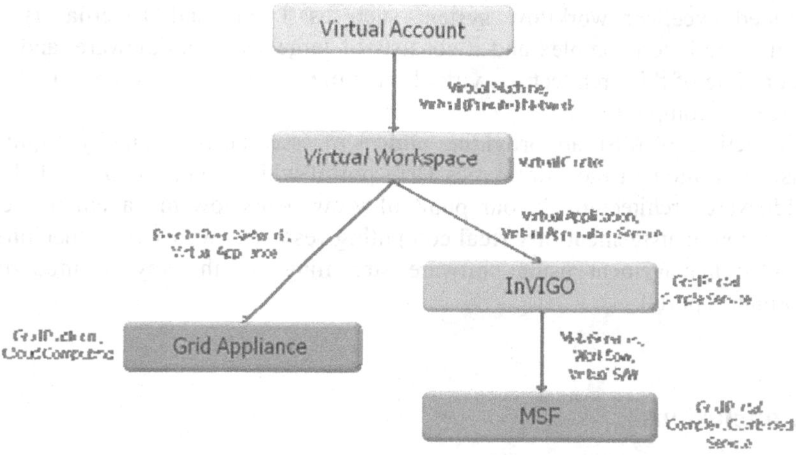

Fig. 4. Comparision of MSF to Functionalities and Related Resource Virtualization

Virtual workspace increased flexibility of Grid computing resources with virtual machine technology. Virtual workspace is constructed using virtual machines and virtual private network connecting the virtual machines. By using a private network of virtual machines, virtual computing resource dedicated virtually on a user and isolated from other user is defined. Virtual workspace is thought as a private virtual cluster for a Grid user.

Grid Appliance extends extensibility of Grid resource with peer to peer network and user can easily use a virtual appliance. Virtual appliance is a preconfigured and "plug and play" virtual machine that meets user's need. Operating system and software installed in the virtual machine images and it can be used as easily as appliance such as a TV or a refrigerator. The only thing user to do is just boot a virtual machine images. Virtual machine consisting work node of the MSF is also thought as a virtual appliance. In the Grid appliance, a virtual appliance called "grid appliance" is distributed and if user execute the virtual appliance, the virtual machine connected to Grid Appliance with virtual peer to peer networks and user could use resources provided by Grid Appliance easily. Grid Appliance provides a Grid platform that called Cloud computing recently.

InVIGO metioned previous section of our paper uses whole virtualization concept that virtualize anything used in Grid Computing such as machines, data, networks, applications and etc. Especially the virtual application concept provided wrapping of legacy application and transforming the legacy application into multiple virtual applications that having various parameter and functionality. It is a ideal concept that integrating legacy application to a Grid portal with resource virtualization, but it lacks workflow functionalities. Workflow functionalities are very essential in the bio informatics Grid portal.

There are many state of the art grid middleware architecture can be used to construct a bio informatics Grid portal such as GridLab and myGrid. They also provided excellent workflow system such as Triana and Taverna. But this architecture is too complex and it consists of large set of middleware, and in the design time of this architecture, virtual machine technologies are not widely used in the Grid computing.

Objectives of MSF are providing almost of essential functionality required to construct a modern bio informatics Grid portal with a light weight and flexible middleware architecture. In our point of view, workflow management, service integration, management of virtual computing resources with virtual machine and software management using software streaming are the key of modern bio informatics portal.

6 Conclusions

In this paper, we present a Grid middleware framework which supports for a workflow model based on virtualized resources. This framework is proposed to overcome the limitation of virtual application using Meta Services. In this framework, Meta Services exposes workflow as a portal service and service call is converted different workflow according to parameter and workflow generated by the Meta Services is scheduled in a virtual cluster which configured by this framework. Because of virtual application service can be composed of workflow and service interface wraps the workflow providing a complex portal services composed by small application could effectively integrated to Grid portal and scheduled in virtual computing resources.

Reference

1. M. Jankowskil, P. Wolniewiczl, J. Denemark, N. Meyer, and L. Matyska, "Virtual Environments – Framework for Virtualized Resource Access in the Grid," LNCS 4375 – Euro-Par 2006: Parallel Processing, pp.101-111, Springer, 2007.
2. K. Keahey, I. Foster, T. Freeman, and X. Zhang, "Virtual Workspace: Achieveing Quality of Service and Quality of Life in the Grid," Scientific Programming Journal, 2006.

Grid Workflow-Driven Healthcare Platform for Collaborative Heart Disease Simulator

Chan-Hyun Youn*, Hoeyoung Kim*, Dong Hyun Kim*, Wooram Jung*, and Eun Bo Shim**

School of Engineering, Information and Communications University,

119, Munjiro, Yuseong-gu, Daejeon, 305-732, Korea*

Department of Mechanical & Biomedical Engineering, Kangwon National University Hyoja-dong, Chuncheon, Kangwon 200-701, Korea **

{chyoun}@icu.ac.kr*, ebshim@kangwon.ac.kr**

Abstract: This paper proposes a policy adjuster-driven Grid workflow management system, which supports collaborative heart disease diagnosis applications. To select policies according to service level agreement of users and dynamic resource status, we devised a policy adjuster to negotiate workflow management polices and resource management policies using policy decision scheme.

1. Introduction

Grid resource management systems [1] provide better resource selection for applications based on dynamic resource status and different theoretical scheduling algorithms. However, the complexity of resource management for QoS guarantee in Grid significantly increases as the grid computing grows. One of the promising approaches trying to solve this problem is policy based resource management system [2] that is suitable to the complex management environments. To manage resource in Grid, it is required to have a sort of grid resource broker and scheduler that manage resources and jobs in the virtual Grid environment. [3] suggested policy-based resource management system (PQRM) architecture based on Grid Service Level Agreement (SLA) and abstract architecture of grid resource management.

Since collaboration is becoming emphasized in many fields, healthcare platform is becoming more important; in practical clinical medical field, the importance of system for collaboration between doctors or researchers is also increasing.

In medical healthcare environment, beside most of single-program applications, which have only one sequential or parallel program, there exist many applications

O.-H. Byeon et al. (eds.), *Future Application and Middleware Technology on e-Science*,
DOI 10.1007/978-1-4419-1719-5_10,

which require co-process of many programs following a strict processing order. Since these applications are executed on Grid, they are called Grid workflows. Current Grid resource management systems do not consider complexity of collaborative medical applications and service level guarantee at workflow level. So this paper proposes Grid workflow-driven healthcare platform for collaborative applications and implement workflow-Integrated PQRM as one instance for this workflow-driven healthcare platform. We discuss the performance of the proposed workflow-driven healthcare platform by measuring the completion time of collaborative heart disease simulator under different user SLA.

2. Model Description of Grid Workflow-Driven Healthcare Platform

2.1. Architecture of PQRM based workflow-driven healthcare platform

To provide optimum job scheduling solutions based on users' SLA for collaborative heart disease care services, we propose a new architecture of Grid workflow-driven healthcare platform with policy adjuster integrated based on PQRM system [5]. To adjust different policies according to the requirements in SLA, policy adjuster is developed to manage resource mapping policies for sub-jobs in the workflow. To handle each application in environment processing huge amount of data and signal, we adopt policy quorum based resource management technologies and design this system to manage job execution and heterogeneous resources.

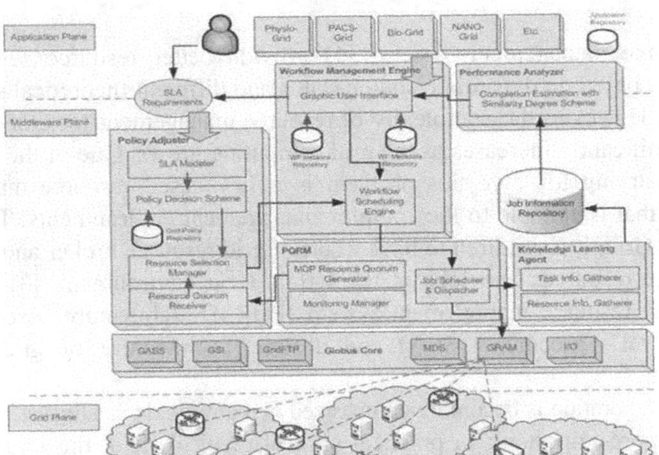

Fig. 1. Architecture of Grid workflow-driven healthcare platform with policy adjuster integrated

Fig. 1 shows layered architecture of policy adjuster integrated workflow management system for collaborative healthcare services. Doctors and patients build their applications of collaborative healthcare services in the graphic user interface.

Performance analyzer provides the prediction finish time for the collaborative healthcare services using completion estimation with similarity degree scheme by analyzing the historical data. According to the prediction information, users can set up their SLA requirements. The application requests are then submitted and parsed into tasks and dependencies in workflow management engine. Policy adjuster analyzes the input SLA and maps the tasks of workflow in time using policy decision algorithm to achieve the optimized mapping solution in terms of the SLA requirements. After receiving the mapping information from policy adjuster, workflow scheduling engine allocates tasks to resources and creates task managers to manage and monitor the tasks. PQRM components are responsible to monitor the resource status, generate the Available Resource Quorum (ARQ) and dispatch the jobs in Grid environment

Main functions in our system are listed as follows:

- *Workflow Scheduling Engine*: is a manager for the tasks in the workflow to allocate each task to the specific resource selected by policy adjuster and monitor the job execution status in its lifetime.
- *Policy Decision Scheme*: receives SLA constrains from users and determines a specific system policy using in this execution for all the workflow sub-jobs to find a best mapping solution according to users' intention.
- *Completion Estimation with Similarity Degree Scheme*: receives the task name and the resource as input, analyzes the historical executions and predicts the probable runtime of the next execution.

Comparing with general workflow management systems [17], our proposing system is more advanced and efficient in the following aspects. Firstly, we provide many advanced functions for collaborative healthcare services such as geometry poincare analyzer and 3-D virtual heart simulator; secondly, future runtime of a job can be predicted in our system using completion estimation with similarity degree algorithm by analyzing the historical data; thirdly, the execution status of each task on Grid resource can be monitoring and shown to users; finally, SLA requirements of users can be guaranteed by adjusting policies. Users can select time optimized execution policy or cost optimized execution policy as their intentions.

2.2. Service Scenario of Collaborative Healthcare Platform

In this section, a medical scenario shows how a physician might treat a patient to identify the heart disease by collecting the information from ECG analysis and simulating the data using Virtual Heart Simulator. The service description of advanced ECG processing and Virtual Heart Simulation is shown in a scenario of fig. 2

The application begins when a patient goes to the doctor with heart disease suspicion. Firstly, doctor acquires ECG signals by sensing the heart bit rate of the patient. If high (HR>110 [BPM]) or low heart rates (HR<60 [BPM]) is detected, medical doctor needs to ask the SRI questions to find heart rate related stress factors for more detailed and accurate diagnosis. He may also need to the collaborative diagnosis with other medical doctors on this symptom. The sensitivity analysis of poincare geometry-characteristics with PP and RR index ratio is processed. The transmitted SRI responses and ECG signals are stored at the databases in medical centers. Then if there are patients' or any customer's heart rate changes, medical doctors may start identification process whether major factor is mental stress, heart disease, or arrhythmia from regression analysis.

Based on the ECG processing, doctor decides to utilize the Virtual heart simulation to virtualize the ECG sensing data stored in the database of medical centers. The computing of virtual heart simulation would be separated in the distributed heterogeneous resources in the Grid environment.

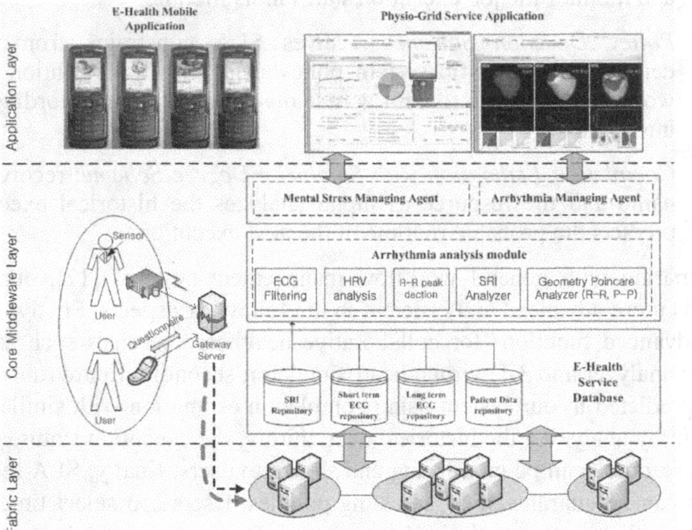

Fig. 2. Service description of advance ECG processing and Virtual Heart Simulation

Before the medical doctor executes collaborative healthcare application in our workflow-driven platform, he may need to set up the requirements for different service levels in SLA such as time optimized service or cost optimized service. In our workflow management system, we are now considering two main factors: finish time and cost. We set $SLA = \{ft, co\}$, where $0 \le ft,\ co \le 1$. Each factor has a real number value, and the closer one value means the higher intent factor in SLA for a user.

In this scenario, the doctor wants to get the visualized result of virtual heart as soon as possible, so he sets the *ft* to 1. Then a suitable policy is selected by policy adjuster to guarantee the fastest finish time. Finally, the result of simulation is provided to doctors. In this way, patients with heart disease can receive more visualized and accurate diagnosis in the minimal time.

3. Implementation and Evaluation

We evaluate policy adjuster-driven workflow management system's performance by using a collaborative health disease identification application. We evaluate the general system, PQRM system[5] and our proposed policy adjuster-driven workflow management under different user's SLA types. The general system submits the job randomly because it does not consider resource management. PQRM system use allocation cost to select the resources. Policy Adjuster-driven workflow management system has three submission strategies: Finish Time Optimization, Cost Optimization and mapping considering both Time and Cost together. Policy adjuster is used to differentiate policies for those different submission strategies. The sub jobs will be mapped to our resource pool based on different scheduling policies. We monitor the completion time of job and resource cost under these three different systems.

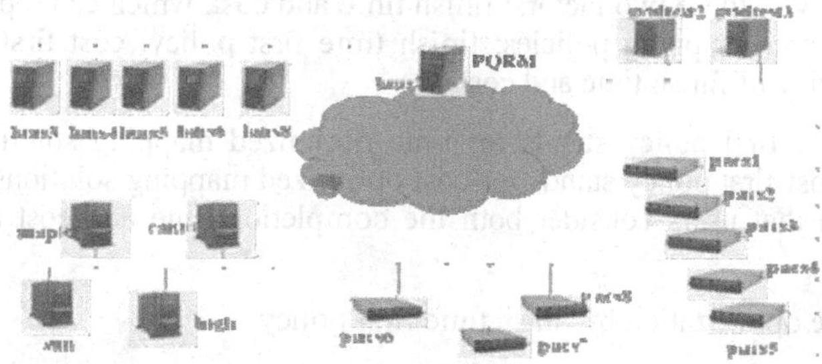

Fig. 3. Expriment Network Topology

As shown in fig. 3, in our experiment environment there are several different types of resources. lans series resources are high performance HP cluster machines; pacs 1-5 series resources are general IBM servers; pacs 6-8 are high performance IBM servers with high price; gridtest resources are general desktop computers with low price; maple, canna, sun and high are high performance duo-core cluster machines. Table 1 shows the detail description of resources.

As listed in table 1, In general workflow system, there is no SLA guarantee mechanism and best effort mapping solution is used. In PQRM system, allocation cost is used as a metric to select the optimal resources.

Table 1. List of SLA Types with related Policies

System	SLA strategy		Policy	Note
	Finish time	Cost		
General Workflow System	-	-	-	Best effort
PQRM System	-	-	-	Allocation cost optimization
Policy Adjuster integrated Workflow Management System	1	0	Finish Time First Policy	Time optimization
	0	1	Cost First Policy	Cost optimization
	0.1	0.9	Combined Policy of Finish time and cost	Care cost much more than finish time
	0.3	0.7		Care cost a little more than finish time
	0.5	0.5		Care cost and finish time as the same importance
	0.7	0.3		Care finish time a little more than cost
	0.9	0.1		Care finish time much more than cost

In our proposed system, since the value of SLA factor is from 0 to 1, we use a form of SLA with these two factors: finish time and cost, which can represent three different resource mapping policies: finish time first policy, cost first policy and combined policy of finish time and cost.

Finish time first policy stands for time optimized mapping solutions; on the other hand, cost first policy stands for cost optimized mapping solutions; combined policy means that users consider both the completion time and cost at the same time.

- Time optimization by finish time first policy

Time optimization is an important service type that can provide shortest execution time for the applications. When the finish time factor in SLA is set to 1, the finish time first policy is selected to achieve time optimization execution for this application. As shown in fig. 4, we measure the total execution time of ECG application under four different strategies.

In the experiment, we measure the total execution time of the application which runs on different systems. The broken line stands for the execution time in general workflow management system without any resource mapping policy. The green value is the finish time of PQRM system. Apparently, when we use finish time first policy to execution the application, we can achieve the shortest finish time comparing with other three cases. Cost first policy using in our system has the worst finish time because the costless resources are selected in the executions.

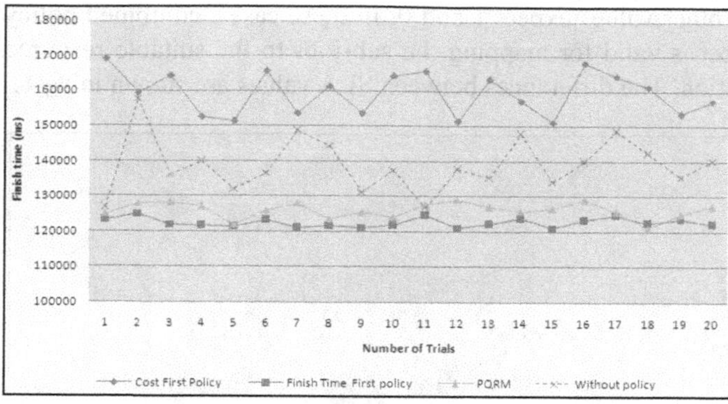

Fig. 4. Completion Time of different policies

- Cost optimization by cost first policy

Cost optimization is another service type in our proposed system. When the cost factor in SLA is set to 1, the cost first policy is selected by our system to achieve cost optimization execution for this application.

As shown in fig. 5, we measure the total cost of the application which runs on different systems. Apparently, cost first policy achieves the lowest average cost for the applications. It can reduce approximate 24% of cost comparing to the PQRM system which consumes highest cost among all the situations. That is because, with cost first policy, users care about cost only, the costless resources in the resource pool are selected. On the other hand, the cost of finish time first policy is much higher than the case without policy.

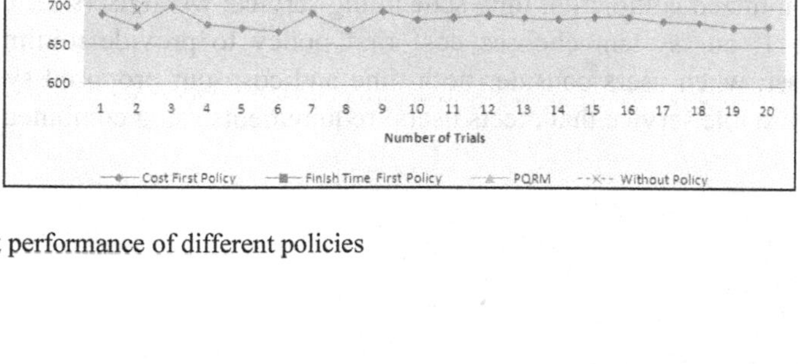

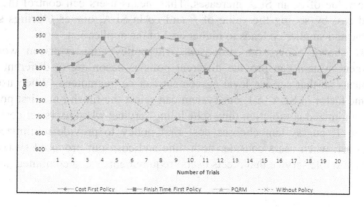

Fig. 5. Cost performance of different policies

- Consider both finish time and cost by combined policy

Besides time optimization and cost optimization strategies, users can construct other SLA types in our proposed system by setting the finish time factor and cost factor with other values expect 1 and 0. In these cases, combined policy of finish time and cost is valid for mapping the sub-jobs to the suitable resources to meet users' intention. The differences between SLA values are shown in fig. 6.

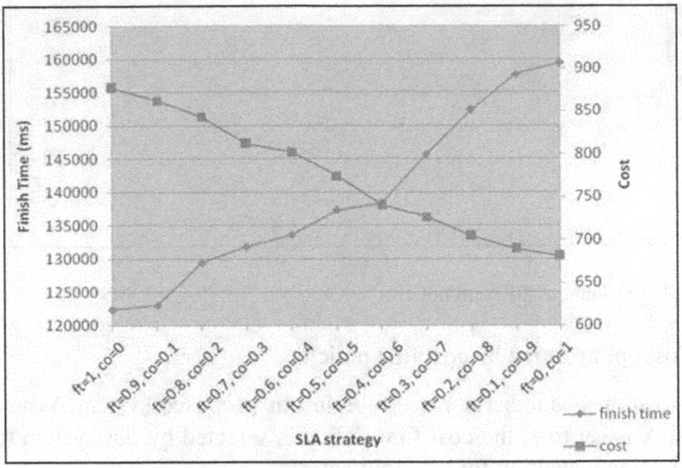

Fig. 6. Finish time and cost under different SLA strategies

Different values of *ft* and *co* stand for the way user evaluates the finish time and cost. The higher value of *ft* means user cares finish time more than cost, the higher value of *co* means user care cost more than finish time. As we can see, when the *ft* value in SLA is decreasing, the finish time of the application is increasing from 122000 to almost 160000. At the same time, the cost is decreasing since the value of *co* in SLA increases. That means users can control the finish time and cost by setting the value of *ft* and *co* in SLA, bigger *ft* brings shorter finish time and smaller *co* leads to higher cost of the application.

As we shown above, our proposed Grid policy adjuster-driven workflow management system can provide different policies according to different users' requirements so that service level agreement can be guaranteed. When users set finish time factor in SLA to 1, our system can select the finish time first policy to provide minimized completion time scheduling service; when users set cost factor in SLA to 1, our system chooses cost first policy to provide minimized cost resources set; when users consider both time and cost, our proposed system also can provide stable service that meets users' requirements using combined policy.

4. Summary

This paper proposes a policy adjuster-driven workflow management system for healthcare platform, which supports collaborative health disease identification applications. To guarantee the SLA of users' requirements, we implemented a new architecture that integrates workflow functions with policy adjuster based on policy quorum based resource management system. We derived a policy adjuster to handle workflow management polices and resource management policies. Based on policy decision scheme, resource selection can be controlled according to service level agreement of users and dynamic resource status. We evaluate this platform through a collaborative heart disease identification application and compare the performance to that of the general workflow system and PQRM system under different types of SLA. The result shows that time optimization can be achieved by finish time first policy and the cost can be reduced by approximate 24% comparing to PQRM system when the cost first policy is used. When the combined policy is adopted, users can control the finish time and cost by setting the factor values in SLA. Therefore the proposed management system can guarantee quality of service for workflow applications based on different user's requirement and dynamic resource status

ACKNOWLEDGEMENT This research was supported in part by the ITRC program and IT R&D program of MKE/IITA [2008-C1090-0801-0014 and 2008-F-029-01].

REFERENCES

[1] K Krauter, R Buyya, M Maheswaran, "Taxonomy of Resource Management in Grid", Software Practice and Experience, 2002

[2] K Yang, A Galis, C Todd, "Policy-based active Grid management architecture", ICON 2002. 10th IEEE International

[3] Dong Su Nam et al., "QoS-constraint Quorum Management scheme for a Grid-based Electrocardiogram", LNCS 3043 pp.352-359, 2004.

[4] Eun Bo Shim et al., "Development of a 3D virtual heart including the mechanism of human cardiac cell physiology-electric conduction of cardiac tissue-heart mechanics", The Korean Society of Mechanical Engineers 60th anniversary fall conference 2005, The Korean Society of Mechanical Engineers, pp58-58, 2005.

[5] Sang-Il Lee, YoungJoo Han, Hyewon Song, Changhee Han, Chan-Hyun Youn, "Grid Policy Administrator with MDP-Based Resource Management Scheme", Proc. The 2006 Int. Conf. on Grid Computing & Applications, pp. 25-31, June 2006

[6] T. Oinn, M. Addis, J. Ferris, D. Marvin, M. Senger, M. Greenwood, T. Carver and K. Glover, M.R. Pocock, A. Wipat, and P. Li, "Taverna: a tool for the composition and enactment of bioinformatics workflows". Bioinformatics, 20(17):3045-3054, Oxford University Press, London, UK, 2004.
[7] Ian J. Taylor et al., "Workflows for e-Science", chap. 13. Oxford: Clarendon, 1892, pp.190–191.
[8] T. Tannenbaum, D. Wright, K. Miller, and M. Livny, "Condor - A Distributed Job Scheduler", Beowulf Cluster Computing with Linux, The MIT Press, MA, USA, 2002.
[9] J Yu, R Buyya 1, "A Taxonomy of Scientific Workflow Systems for Grid Computing", Workflow in Grid Systems Workshop, GGF-10, Berlin, March 9, 2004
[10] Christos G. Cassandras, "Discrete Event Systems: Modeling and Performance Analysis", Aksen Associates Incorporated Publishers, 1993.
[11] www.accessgrid.org
[12] http://www.anl.gov/Media_Center/logos21-2/grid.htm
[13] http://www.library.uams.edu/accessgrid/aghome.aspx
[14] http://cci.uchicago.edu/projects/abc/
[15] L.Altintas et al., "a framework for the design and reuse of grid workflows," Porc. Scientific Appications of Grid computing, LNCS 3458, Springer, 2005, pp. 119-132
[16] E. Neubauser et al., "Workflow-based grid applications," Future Generation Computer System, Jan. 2006, pp. 6-15
[17] B. Ludäscher, I. Altintas, C. Berkley, D. Higgins, E. Jaeger, M. Jones, E. A. Lee, J. Tao, and Y. Zhao, "Scientific Workflow Management and the KEPLER System". Concurrency and Computation: Practice & Experience, Special Issue on Scientific Workflows, to appear, 2005
[18] Issue on Scientific Workflows, to appear, 2005

An Approach to Multi-Objective Aircraft Design

Daniel Neufeld, Joon Chung, and Kamaran Behdinan

Ryerson University, Toronto, Canada, e-mail: daniel.neufeld@gmail.com
Ryerson University, Toronto, Canada, e-mail: j3chung@ryerson.ca

Abstract Aircraft design is a complex process subject to many competing disciplinary analyses and is constrained by many performance targets, airworthiness requirements, environmental regulations, and many other factors. Designers must explore a broad range of possible decisions to find the best trade-offs between many competing performance goals and design constraints while ensuring that the resulting design complies with certification and airworthiness standards. A modular Multi-Disciplinary Optimization (MDO) framework is being developed with the ability to handle multiple simultaneous objectives while considering any airworthiness constraints that can be assessed at the conceptual level. The algorithm implements a multi-objective Genetic Algorithm (GA) within an MDO framework. The problem consists of four core disciplinary analysis including structural weight estimation, aerodynamics, performance, and stability

1 Introduction

Traditional aircraft conceptual design rapidly establishes basic aircraft geometry and engine thrust requirements by considering a few basic performance constraints such as field length, speed, and altitude. These are often calculated by direct solution of simplified analytical equations. Detailed calculation of flight performance and aircraft stability is typically carried out only after the basic aircraft geometry has been established [1]. This can lead to sub-optimal designs or costly revision if the concept proves to be infeasible later in the design process. Ultimately, the certifiability of a design can only be verified by rigorous flight and structural testing and no computational method implemented during design can guarantee success. However, considering airworthiness constraints as early as possible in the design process promises to reduce the likelihood of costly design revisions beyond the conceptual level [2]

O.-H. Byeon et al. (eds.), *Future Application and Middleware Technology on e-Science*,
DOI 10.1007/978-1-4419-1719-5_11, © Springer Science+Business Media, LLC 2010

In addition to current regulations, growing concern regarding the environmental footprint of air travel is leading to new regulations that target aircraft noise and pollutant emissions as well as contrail formation [3]. As a consequence, the software framework is designed with the flexibility to enforce new constraints at any phase in the flight profile to quickly accommodate new and changing regulations and predict the impact they will have on aircraft conceptual design. The optimization problem was divided along traditional aerospace disciplines: aerodynamics, structures, performance, and stability. Several MDO schemes were considered including the Collaborative Optimization (CO) and Multidisciplinary Feasible (MDF) methods both of which have been demonstrated to be effective in aircraft conceptual design optimization [4].

2 Airworthiness

Airworthiness regulations are sets of rules that an aircraft must comply with prior to entering service. The rules cover detailed performance requirements for normal operation and operation under engine failure scenarios, structural safety factors, passenger ergonomics, access to emergency exits, fail safe avionics, and many others. Many of these regulations cannot be determined at the conceptual design level. However, enforcing the ones that can be determined will help prevent the optimization process from generating ideal but impractical designs [2]. The regulations enforced in this research include balanced field length (takeoff with engine failure), single engine climb rates, reserve fuel for diversions to alternate airports, Extended Twin Engine Operations (ETOPS), passenger head room, and access to emergency exits.

Some of these regulations are enforced explicitly by implementing design rules that use regulations to calculate a feasible configuration. For example, landing gear positions are explicitly calculated such that ground stability rules are accommodated. Regulations such as initial climb rate, stall speed and stability are constrained implicitly by the optimizer. When the performance of a candidate design is calculated, any violation of the certification rules contributes to a penalty value which is constrained by the optimizer to vanish by the end of the optimization.

3 Methodology

Traditional aircraft design evaluates disciplines sequentially and iteratively. Due to the high degree disciplinary coupling, predicting the influence of design changes in one discipline on another can be exceedingly difficult [1]. MDO ensures that disciplines can be simultaneously optimized by implementing one of the many available methods. In this research, the aircraft design problem was decomposed into four disciplines. Disciplinary coupling was handled by the implementing the Multidisciplinary Feasible (MDF) approach to MDO using a multi-objective GA optimizer.

3.1 Problem Formulation

The optimization problem was divided along traditional aerospace disciplines: aerodynamics, structures, performance, and stability. The problem consists of both discrete and continuous design variables and a coarse design space due to the flight simulation approach to aircraft performance analysis. While gradient based optimizers like Sequential Quadratic Programming (SQP) are generally more efficient than stochastic algorithms, they can encounter significant difficulties when solving coarse functions or truly discrete design variables [5, 6]. Stochastic methods do not require gradient information and are therefore much less sensitive to coarse functions and can handle discrete design variables without difficulty. Additionally, population based optimizers such as GAs are particularly suited for solving multiobjective problems [7].

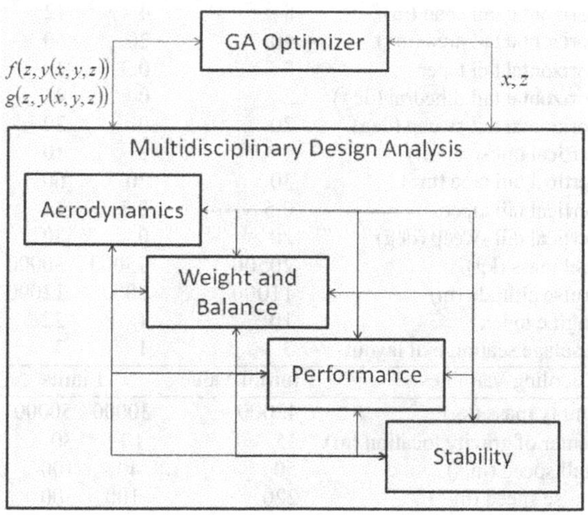

Fig. 1. Simplified algorithm block diagram.

The MDO architecture implements the MDF method. This architecture consists of a single optimizer coupled with a Multidisciplinary Analysis (MDA) algorithm. The optimizer operates on the design variables while the MDA algorithm ensures that all coupling variables are consistent across each discipline by solving each discipline analysis with estimated coupling variable values and iterating until all of the discrepancies vanish.

The MDF architecture has the advantage that all candidate designs generated by the optimizer are feasible across all disciplines. Some multi-level methods only guarantee feasibility when the optimization has completed. MDF can become impractical when there are a large number of coupling variables [4, 8]. However, the MDF method works both efficiently and reliably on the problem presented in this research. A simplified block diagram of the algorithm is shown in figure 1. The design variables and coupling variables are shown in table 1. The initial values were assigned to produce a starting point similar to the Airbus A320-200, a typical regional airliner with a 160 passenger capacity. The limits were set to a 20% margin above and below the initial values to give a wide search space. The example that is further discussed in the Results section.

Table 1. Design and coupling variables and limits

Design Variables	Initial Value	Limits	
wing span (m)	34	25	35
wing area (m^2)	120	100	200
wing taper ratio	0.5	0.3	1
wing dihedral (deg)	2	0	4
wing sweep (deg)	25	0	30
horizontal tail span (m)	8	4	12
horizontal tail area (m^2)	40	20	60
horizontal tail taper	0.5	0.3	1
horizontal tail dihedral (deg)	2	0	4
horizontal tail sweep (deg)	20	0	30
vertical tail span (m)	4	2	10
vertical tail area (m^2)	30	20	60
vertical tail taper	0.5	0.3	1
vertical tail sweep (deg)	20	0	30
fuel mass (kg)	20500	15000	30000
cruise altitude (m)	11000	5000	12000
engine index	10	1	22
fuselage seating/exit layout	3	1	7
Coupling Variables	**Initial Value**	**Limits**	
empty mass (kg)	42000	30000	50000
center of gravity location (m)	15	10	30
stall speed (m/s)	50	40	100
cruise speed (m/s)	220	100	300
lift slope (1/rad)	5	4	7
maximum lift coefficient	1.5	0.5	2
drag coefficient	0.02	0.01	0.1
induced drag constant	0.005	0.001	0.01
aerodynamic neutral point (m)	15	10	20
moments of inertia (Ix, Iy, Iz)	-	-	-
aircraft stability derivatives	-	-	-

3.2 Automated Design

The set of design variables generated by the optimizer is not sufficient to compute all aspects of the dimensions, layout, and performance of an aircraft design. A set of configuration rules was developed to determine the unknown properties of each aircraft design given the design variables. These rules determine the location of the engines, the location, size, and available capacity of the fuel tanks, the position and size of the landing gear, and the layout of the fuselage. Some of the rules were developed by implementing some common aircraft design 'rules of thumb' and others were developed by enforcing certification requirements.

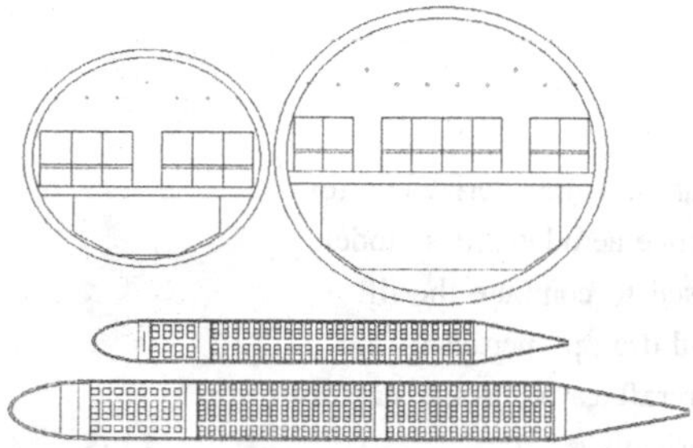

Fig. 2. Fuselage layout examples. Optimized seating arrangement is shown with aisle widths, passenger headroom, and exit proximity rules enforced. Configurations for small regional aircraft to large wide-body jets can be generated.

The fuselage circumference is optimized by searching for a configuration that accommodates airworthiness regulations for passenger headroom, aisle width, and exit proximity while leaving sufficient space for standard sized cargo containers. This allows the optimizer to influence the slenderness of the fuselage without creating impractical configurations. The location of the aisles and exits are determined by complying with regulations for passenger access. Figure 2 shows the output of the fuselage design algorithm for a small regional jet and a large wide-body aircraft. Figure 3 shows an example of a fully configured design.

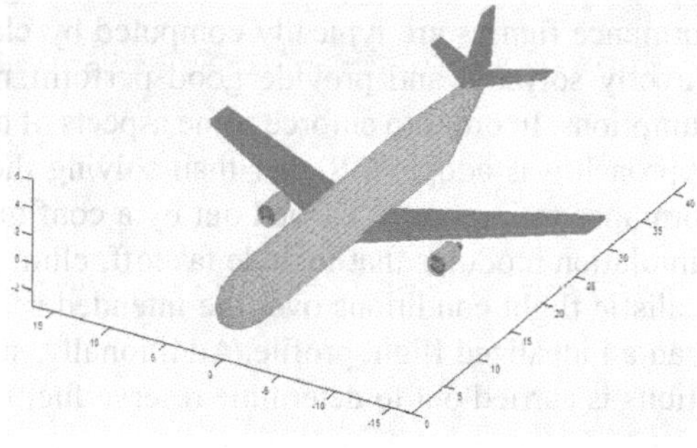

Fig. 3. Successive MDA iterations ensure design variable consistency resulting in a complete aircraft model and projected performance, weight, stability, and aerodynamic properties.

3.3 Aerodynamics Discipline

The aerodynamics disciplinary analysis is based on a non-planar, subsonic vortex lattice solver with a compressibility correction and a detailed set of semi-empirical equations to estimate the parasite drag contribution of each component of the aircraft. The vortex lattice method is a classical computational method for computing flow properties and aerodynamic forces [9]. The parameterized aerodynamics model is shown in fig. 4. The method is significantly faster and easier to implement than Computational Fluid Dynamics (CFD) and provides a sufficient degree of accuracy, flexibility, and speed for conceptual aircraft design. The aerodynamics discipline solves for induced drag, parasite drag, lift and drag coefficients, aerodynamic center, and stability derivatives given the aircraft geometry and flight conditions.

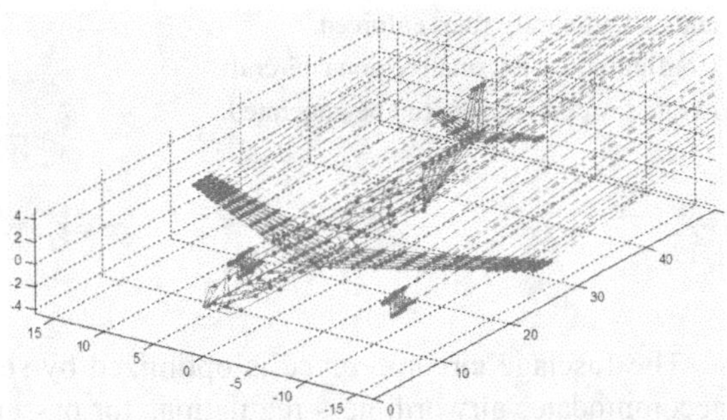

Fig. 4. Parameterized vortex lattice aerodynamics model. Used to compute the lift and drag properties of the aircraft as well as the stability derivatives.

3.4 Performance Discipline

The performance discipline calculates the performance characteristics of a proposed aircraft design. These figures include takeoff distance, climb performance, altitude capabilities, cruise range, descent, and landing. In aircraft conceptual design, performance figures are typically computed by classical analytical equations that are directly solvable and provide good performance estimates given some ideal assumptions. In order to enforce some aspects of airworthiness regulations, a different approach was adopted. Rather than solving the analytical equations directly, performance estimation is carried out by a configurable set of two-dimensional flight simulation modules that include takeoff, climb, cruise, descent, and landing under realistic flight conditions over the intended route of the new aircraft design rather than an idealized flight profile. Additionally, simulation of contingency flight situations is carried out to determine reserve fuel requirements and flight performance requirements under engine failure. The realistic flight profile simulated by the performance discipline is shown in fig. 5.

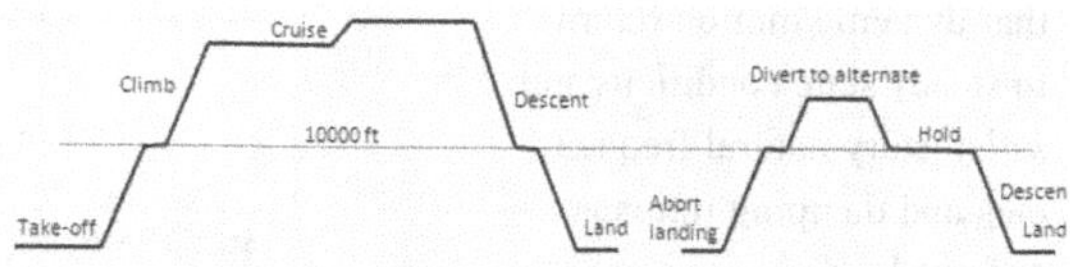

Fig. 5. Airworthy route profile. Aircraft performance is evaluated by simulation of an air-traffic compliant route. Reserve fuel is computed by simulating a contingency scenario.

The optimization objectives are driven by the aircraft performance over an entire route rather than single performance figures like range or cruise speed. Typical objectives may be minimizing block time, minimizing block fuel consumption, or maximizing block distance. Introducing contingency performance constraints enhances the probability of design certifiability by adding additional pressure to the optimization scheme to develop aircraft with acceptable single engine missed approach performance and climb rate, and single engine cruise capability optimized simultaneously with the main objective function. Additionally, if the design route requires flight operations into airports with no nearby alternates, a desired diversion range can be enforced according to the Extended-range Twin-engine Operational Performance Standards (ETOPS).

Engine performance is computed by interpolating engine manufacturer data held in a database. These data are accessed by a discrete design variable indicating a specific engine in the database. The data is imported and interpolated over the airspeeds and altitudes required by the simulation modules.

3.5 Stability Discipline

Dynamic stability constraints can have a significant effect on the design of the empennage and wing shape, but is often not considered in the conceptual design phase [10, 11]. The stability discipline solves the linearized aircraft equations of motion to estimate the dynamic response of each aircraft concept to ensure that the aircraft returns to steady flight after a disturbance. Additionally, handling qualities of the aircraft are constrained so that the optimized conceptual designs will comply with both the certification regulations and with subjective handling quality guidelines, shown in fig. 6.

Frequency and damping ratios for both short and long period motions in both the lateral and longitudinal modes are determined and checked for instability or poor handling quality. If any mode is found to be in violation of the stability or handling criteria, they contribute to a penalty value which is minimized by the optimizer.

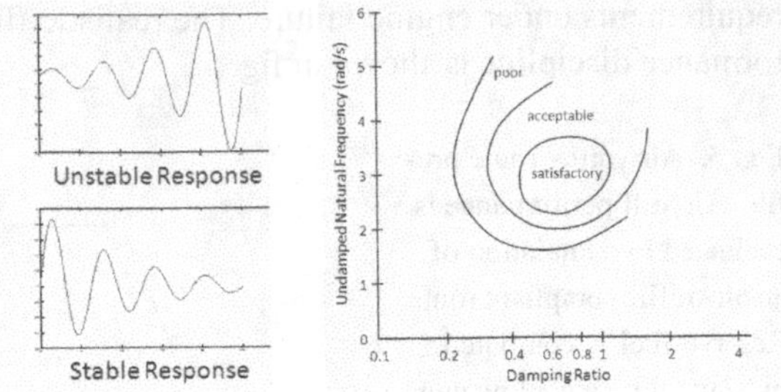

Fig. 6. Stable dynamic responses are enforced for both lateral and longitudinal modes. The constraints ensure that dynamic motion returns to steady state conditions and satisfactory natural frequencies and damping ratios are enforced

4 Results

A multi-objective optimization problem was developed to illustrate the design optimization of a mid-sized, narrow-body regional aircraft having 160 passengers. The flight profile of the aircraft including the cruise speed and altitude was permitted to be adjusted by the optimizer to show the trade off between aggressive and conservative performance targets on aircraft conceptual designs. The optimization objectives and constraints are shown in table 2.

Table 2. Example objectives and constraints

Objectives	Goal
Block time	minimize
Block fuel	minimize

Performance Constraints	Goal
Static margin	>5%
Takeoff distance	<200 m
Route distance	≥5000 km
Certification penalty	= 0
Dynamic stability penalty	= 0

The GA was set to run for 100 generations with a population of 35 individuals. The computation time was approximately 16 hours on a quad core computer. A sample of the initial and final populations is shown in fig. 7 to illustrate the evolution of the designs.

The Pareto-optimal solutions are shown in figure 8. As expected, designs with a shorter block time travel at a higher speed with more powerful engines and consume more fuel over the route. The aircraft that take longer to complete the route fly slower with less powerful engines, but consume significantly less fuel. This type of result allows aircraft designers to examine the trade-off between performance targets, enabling them to select a design which has the best possible compromise between competing objectives. Table 3 compares the specifications of each design

Fig. 7. Left: Initial population sample. Right: Final population sample, 100 generations

on the Pareto front. The specifications for the Airbus A320-200, a regional aircraft in a similar size category to the test problem, are also shown for comparison.

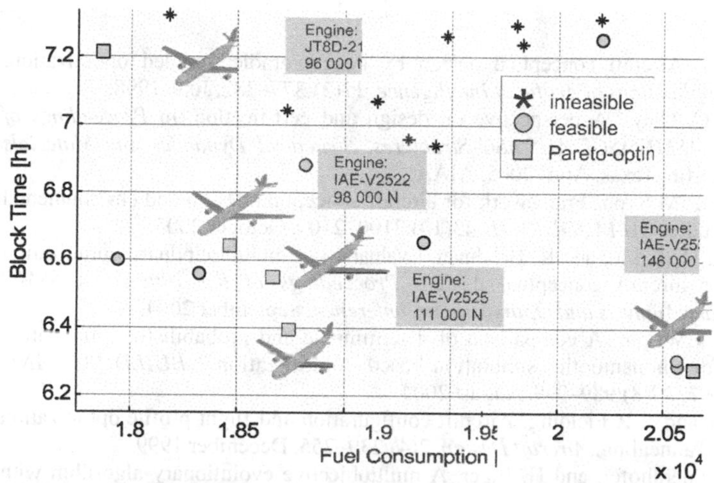

Fig. 8. The Pareto-optimal front shows the trade-off between speed and fuel efficiency.

Table 3. Specifications of Pareto-optimal aircraft conceptual designs.

Specifications	A320-200	Design 1	Design 2	Design 3	Design 4	Design 5
Block Time (h)	-	7.22	6.64	6.54	6.39	6.29
Block Fuel (kg)	29600	17822	18302	18518	18608	20617
Range (km)	5700	5000	5000	5000	5000	5000
Thrust (SSL, lb)	33000	22000	25000	33000	33000	33000
Span (m)	34.1	40	42	42	42	42
Aspect Ratio	10	12	12	13	13	13
Field Length (m)	2000	1700	1820	1535	1572	1536
Cruise Mach	0.78	0.66	0.71	0.72	0.74	0.75
Cruise Alt (ft)	37000	34200	35400	35400	34800	32000
Aisle layout	3+3	3+3	3+3	3+3	3+3	3+3

5 Conclusions

An MDO framework for aircraft conceptual design capable of assessing some certification standards involving dynamic stability and handling qualities, fuselage layout, and aircraft performance was developed. The algorithm implements a multiobjective GA and four disciplinary analyses including performance, stability, weight and balance, and aerodynamics. The results show the trade-off between changing the performance targets for new aircraft in the conceptual design phase. The probability that the resulting conceptual designs are feasible and realistic was enhanced by enforcing some certification standards earlier in the design process than traditional aircraft design.

References

1. A. H. W. Bos. Aircraft conceptual design by genetic/gradient-guided optimization. *Engineering Applications of Artificial Intelligence*, 11(3):377–382, June 1998.
2. D. Veley and C. Clay. A perspective on design and certification. In *Proceedings of the 46th AIAA/ASME/ASCE/AHS/ASC Structures, Structural Dynamics and Materials Conference*, Austin, Texas, April 2005. AIAA.
3. NE Antoine and IM Kroo. Framework for aircraft conceptual design and environmental performance studies. *AIAA JOURNAL*, 43(10):2100–2109, October 2005.
4. R. E. Perez, H. H. T. Liu, and K. Behdinan. Evaluation of multidisciplinary optimization approaches for aircraft conceptual design. *Proceedings of the 10th AIAA/ISSMO Multidisciplinary Analysis and Optimization Conference*, September 2004.
5. M Wetter and J Wright. A comparison of deterministic and probabilistic optimization algorithms for nonsmooth simulation-based optimization. *BUILDING AND ENVIRONMENT*, 39(8):989–999, August 2004.
6. Rajkumar Pant and J. P. Fielding. Aircraft configuration and flight profile optimization using simulated annealing. *Aircraft Design*, 2(4):239–255, December 1999.
7. H. Langer, T. Puehlhofer, and H. Baier. A multiobjective evolutionary algorithm with integrated response surface functionalities for configuration optimization with discrete variables. *Proceedings 10th AIAA/ISSMO Multidisciplinary Analysis and Optimization Conference*, 30(01.09), 2004.
8. S. Yi, J. Shin, and G. Park. Comparison of mdo methods with mathematical examples. *Structural and Multidisciplinary Optimization*, 35(5):391–402, May 2008.
9. P Konstadinopoulos, DF Thrasher, DT Mook, AH Nayfeh, and L Watson. A vortex-lattice method for general, unsteady aerodynamics. *Journal of Aircraft*, 22(1):43–49, 1985.
10. SJ Morris and I Kroo. Aircraft design optimization with dynamic performance constraints. *Journal of Aircraft*, 27(12):1060–1067, December 1990.
11. B Chudoba, G Coleman, H Smith, and MV Cook. Generic stability and control for aerospace flight vehicle conceptual design. *AERONAUTICAL JOURNAL*, 112(1132):293–306, June 2008.

Experiences and Requirements for Interoperability Between HTC and HPC-driven e-Science Infrastructure

Morris Riedel, Achim Streit, Daniel Mallmann, Felix Wolf and Thomas Lippert

Morris Riedel, Co-Chair of Grid Interoperation Now (GIN) Group of the Open Grid Forum (OGF) Ju¨ lich Supercomputing Centre, Forschungszentrum Ju¨ lich GmbH,
e-mail: m.riedel@fz-juelich.de

Abstract. Recently, more and more e-science projects require resources in more than one production e-science infrastructure, especially when using HTC and HPC concepts together in one scientific workflow. But the interoperability of these infrastructures is still not seamlessly provided today and we argue that this is due to the absence of a realistically implementable reference model in Grids. Therefore, the fundamental goal of this paper is to identify requirements that allows for the definition of the core building blocks of an interoperability reference model that represents a trimmed down version of OGSA in terms of functionality, is less complex, more fine-granular and thus easier to implement. The identified requirements are underpinned with gained experiences from world-wide interoperability efforts

1 Introduction

Many applications take already advantage of a wide variety of e-science infrastructures that evolved over the last couple of years to production environments. Along with this evolution we observed still slow adoption of the Open Grid Services Architecture (OGSA) concept originally defined by Foster et al. in 2002 [8]. While OGSA represents a good architectural blueprint for infrastructures in general, we argue that the scope of OGSA is actually to broad to be realistically implementable for today's production e-science infrastructures in particular. This has mainly two reasons. First, the process of developing open standards that are conform to the whole OGSA ecosystem take rather long, including the precise specification of all the interconnections of these services and their adoption by the respective middleware providers. Second, the launch of OGSA-conform components within production e-science infrastructures take rather long. Although some aspects of OGSA are (or become) relevant to the e-science infrastructures

O.-H. Byeon et al. (eds.), *Future Application and Middleware Technology on e-Science*,
DOI 10.1007/978-1-4419-1719-5_12,

(execution management and service oriented concepts), many services are still very inmature (e.g. advance reservation, service level agreements, virtualization, fault detection and recovery) or many concepts have not been widely adopted in Grid middleware technologies (e.g. service lifetime management, service factories, or notification patterns).

The absence of a realistically implementable reference model is diametral to the fundamental design principles of software engineering and has thus lead to numerous different architectures of production e-science infrastructures and their deployed technologies in the past. To provide some examples, the Enabling Grids for e-Science (EGEE) [17] infrastructure uses the gLite middleware, the TeraGrid [21] infrastructure uses the Globus middleware, the Distributed European Infrastructure for Supercomputing Applications (DEISA) [1] uses the UNICORE middleware, the Open Science Grid (OSG) [19] uses the Virtual Data Toolkit (VDT) and NorduGrid [23] uses the ARC middleware. Most elements of these technologies and infrastructures are not interoperable at the time of writing because of limited adoption of open standards and OGSA concepts.

The lack of interoperability is a hinderence since we observe a growing interest in conveniently using more than one infrastructure with one client that use interoperable components in different Grids. Recently, Riedel et al. [10] provided a classification of different approaches of how to use e-science infrastructures. Among simple scripts with limited control functionality, scientific application plugins, complex workflows, and interactive access, there is also infrastructure interoperability mentioned as one approach to perform e-science. Many e-scientists would like to benefit from interoperable e-science infrastructures in terms of having seamless access to a wide variety of different services or resources. In fact many scientific projects raise the demand to access both High Throughput Computing (HTC)-driven infrastructures (e.g. EGEE, OSG) and High Performance Computing (HPC)-driven infrastructures (e.g. DEISA, TeraGrid) with one client technology or Web portal.

Although one goal of OGSA is to facilitate the interoperability of different Grid technologies and infrastructures in e-science and e-business, we state that the requirements for interoperability in e-science infrastructures have to be specified much more precisely than within OGSA. Therefore, this paper defines a set of requirements based on lessons learned obtained from interoperability work between production e-science infrastructures. The goal is to identify a suitable set of requirements to definde the necessary building blocks for a reference model that is much closer oriented towards the interoperability of production e-science infrastructures than OGSA. This reference model should not replace OGSA but rather trim it down in functionality by dropping several parts of it and refining other parts that are mostly relevant to interoperability of e-science infrastructures.

History of computer science shows that often complex architectures were less used than their trimmed down versions. For instance, the complex SGML was less used than its smaller version XML, which was less complex and well-defined and thus fastly become a de-facto standard in Web data processing. Also, the ISO/OSI reference model originally consisted of seven layers, while its much more successful trimmed down version TCP reference model become the de-facto standard in networking. We argue that the same principles can be applied with OGSA by defining a more limited, but more usable reference model. This becomes also increasingly important in the context of economic contraints since the rather huge OGSA requires massive amounts of maintenance while our idea of a reference model should significantly reduce these maintenance costs by providing only a small subset of functionality, but this in a well-defined manner.

This paper is structured as follows. Following the introduction, the scene is set in Section 2 where we list some of our interoperability projects that helped to identify specific requirements for interoperable e-science infrastructures in Section 3. A survey of related work is described in Section 4, while this paper ends with some concluding remarks.

2 Experiences in Interoperability

This section gives insights into several important interoperability projects that provided valuable lessons learned in terms of interoperability between many production e-science infrastructures. Lessons learned and gained experiences out of these projects lay the foundation for our requirement analysis in Section 3.

The OMII-Europe project [5] initially started to work on an e-science infrastructure interoperability use case application of the e-Health community area named as the Wide In Silico Docking on Malaria (WISDOM) project [9]. More recently, this work is continued in DEISA and collaboration with EGEE. The WISDOM project aims to significantly reduce the time and costs in drug development by using in silico drug discovery techniques.

Technically speaking, the overall scientific workflow can be splitted in two parts as described in Riedel et al. [4]. The first part uses the EGEE infrastructure for large in silico docking, which is a computational method for the prediction of whether one molecule will bind to another. This part uses HTC resources in EGEE with so-called embarassingly parallel jobs do not interact with each other. Applications that are used in this part of the workflow are AutoDock and FlexX that are both provided on the EGEE infrastructure. The output of this part is a list of best chemical compounds that might be potential drugs, but do not represent the final solution.

The second part uses the outcome of the first part of the scientific workflow and is concerned with the refinement of the best compound list using molecular dynamics (MD) techniques. For this part, the e-scientists use massively parallel resources in DEISA with the highly scalable AMBER MD package. All in all, the goal of this interoperability application is to accelerate drug discovery using EGEE and DEISA together in the in silico step before performing in vitro experiments.

The framework that enabled the interoperability in this application lead to several job and data management requirements that are listed in the next section. Also, this application can be actually saen as an example for a whole class of interoperability applications that require access to both HTC and HPC resources. Similiar activities within the same class are interoperability efforts performed between the EUFORIA project [7], DEISA, and EGEE. Also e-scientists of the EUFORIA project and thus members of the known ITER community require access to HTC resources (via EGEE) for embarassingly parallel fusion codes and access to HPC resources (via DEISA) for massively parallel fusion codes. The lessons learned from this interoperability project are similiar to the ones in WISDOM, but slightly different in terms of security and workflow settings. This is due to the fact that the e-scientists of EUFORIA would like to use their own Kepler workflow tool.

Other experiences in interoperability have been gained in interoperability work between the EU-IndiaGrid project [11], OMII-Europe, EGEE, and DEISA. The EU-IndiaGrid project works together with specialists of DEISA to enable interoperability between the Indian Grid GARUDA, EGEE and DEISA. Finally, Riedel et al. describes in [2] many different activities of the Grid Interoperation Now (GIN) group of the Open Grid Forum (OGF). All these activities and their lessons learned also contributed to the identification of requirements in the following Section.

3 Requirements for Interoperability

The experiences and lessons learned from numerous international interoperability projects and efforts lead to several specific requirements for the interoperability between HTC- and HPC-driven infrastructures. First and foremost, the cooperation between Grid technology providers (i.e. gLite, Globus, UNICORE, ARC) and deployment teams of different infrastructures (e.g. EGEE, TeraGrid, DEISA, NorduGrid) represents an important social requirement that is often highly underrated. We argue that the right set of people from different Grid technology providers have to sit together with different infrastructure deployment teams to discuss technical problems in order to achieve interoperability in terms of technologies in general and thus of infrastructures in particular. To ensure outreach to the broader Grid community, outcome of this cooperation should be fed back to OGF to encourage discussions in the respective working groups.

To provide an example, Grid deployment teams from the infrastructures EGEE, DEISA and NorduGrid as well Grid technology providers such as gLite, UNICORE, and ARC had a meeting at CERN to discuss how the job exchange interoperability could be significantly improved within Europe. The result of this workshop was given as an input to the OGF GIN group and will be further discussed with related OGF standardization groups.

Technical requirements are illustrated in Figure 1, which indicates that the requirements stated in this section can be found in four different layers. The plumbings for interoperability are orthogonal to all these layers and thus represent a mandatory requirement. The term plumbings refers to the fact that they basically affect any layer significantly although often realized behind the scenes and thus not visible to end users. This section highlights the requirements of the plumbings as well as the job and data management layer. We argue that the network layer is already interoperable mainly through GEANT and thus not considered to be important in our requirement analysis. Furthermore, we state that the different infrastructures and resource layers (i.e. HTC Grid, Cloud, HPC Grid) are given in our analysis as unchangeable elements. In this context, we argue that rather commercial-oriented Clouds like the Amazons Elastic Computing Cloud (E2C) [15] are currently out of the scope of scientific use cases and thus not part of our analysis but listed to provide a complete and realistic picture.

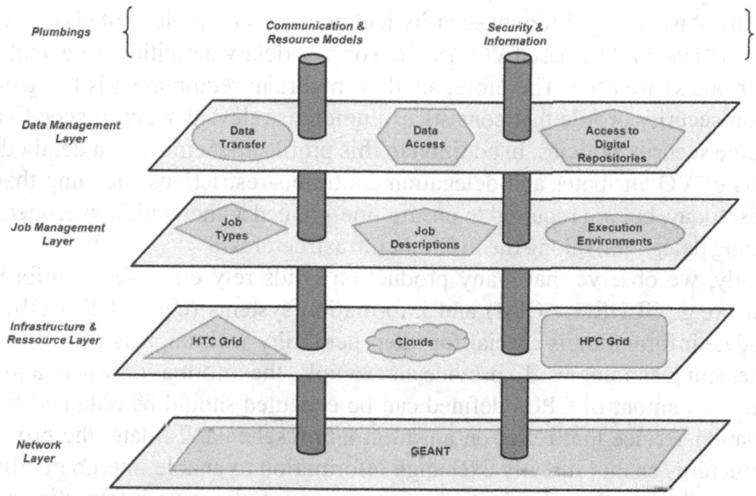

Fig. 1 Interoperablity requirements within four different layers, while two (often behind the scenes realized) plumbings are orthogonal to them because they significantly affect every layer.

3.1 Plumbings

Today, the most production infrastructures use proprietary protocols between their components and thus communication between components of infrastructure A and B is not possible. To provide an example, DEISA deployed UNICORE 5 that uses the proprietary UNICORE Protocol Layer (UPL) [6] for communication. EGEE deployed gLite that also uses proprietary protocols such as the WSMProxy protocol between the User Interface (UI) [20] and Workload Management System (WMS) [20]. Hence, the deployed components of both Grids cannot interact with each other.

As a consequence, the communication technology between major elements must be the same, especially when connecting job and data management technologies of different Grids. The Web services technology based on HTTPS and Simple Object Access Protocol (SOAP) [12] are good foundations to exchange commands and control information, but not to perform large data transfers. In addition, the underlying resource model representation should be compliant with the WS-Resource Framework (WS-RF) [3] or WS-Interoperabiltiy [13] stack to enable common addressing techniques such as WS-Addressing [14].

Even if the communication relies on WS there is still a wide variety of deployed security models in the production infrastructures starting from different certificate types (e.g. full X.509 vs. X.509 proxies) to different delegation techniques (e.g. proxy delegation vs. explicit trust delegation) that do not allow for interoperable applications. Also, many different security technologies are implemented (e.g. VOMS proxies [18] vs. SAML-based VOMS [16]) or proprietary definitions (e.g. authorization attributes) are used. Therefore, another important requirement is to agree on a common security profile that consists of numerous relevant security specifications to enforce security policies. In addition to this profile, there must be a detailed specification of VO attributes and delegation contraints/restrictions encoding that does not exist today, but are required to ensure fine-grained authorization interoperability (including delegation) along the different infrastructures.

Finally, we observe that many production Grids rely on different information schemas (e.g. GLUE vs. CIM) and information systems (e.g. MDS, BDII, CIS). Up-to-date information is crucial for interoperability with impacts on job and data management technologies. To provide an example, the information where a job with a predefined amont of CPUs defined can be executed should be obtained from an information service that relies on an information schema. To date, the production infrastructures cannot directly exchange information to enable interoperability due to different deployed mechanisms. As a consequence, the same information schema (.e.g. GLUE2) must be used in the technologies deployed in the infrastructures. In addition, information services need standard mechanisms to be queried for this kind of information.

3.2 Job Management

Fig. 1 illustrates the job management layer with three different requirement elements. According to the different types of Grids within the infrastructures and resources layer, we also have different types of computational jobs that should be executed on the infrastructures. This in turn leads to the development of different technologies that are used for computational job submission. HTC Grid infrastructures mostly run cycle farming jobs (also named as embarassingly parallel jobs) that do not require a efficient interconnection between the CPUs. As a consequence, middleware packages deployed on these infrastructures (e.g. gLite) use brokering technologies (e.g. WMS) that submit the job on behalf of the user to any free re- source for execution. In contrast, HPC Grid infrastructures mostly run massively parallel jobs that do require an efficient interconnection between cpus and thus cannot be run on any PC pool or similiar farming resource. In turn HPC-driven middleware (e.g. UNICORE) enables end users to manually choose one particular HPC resource due to the general massively-parallel job type, but also because often HPC jobs are even tuned to run on a specific HPC architecture (i.e. memory or network topology requirements). In addition, HPC applications are often compiled on one specific platform and not easy transferable to another. Therefore, we raise the requirement that both cycle farming jobs and massively parallel jobs should be supported in technologies that are deployed on interoperable infrastructures.

Many technologies that are deployed on production Grids still rely on proprietary job description languages derived from the different requirements of the underlying resource infrastructure. In other words it is not possible to exchange jobs directly between different e-science infrastructures although many of the base functionality is the same (e.g. excutable location). To provide an example for different job description languages, TeraGrid deployed Globus, which uses the Resource Specification Language (RSL) [22], DEISA deployed UNICORE, which uses the Abstract Job Object (AJO) [6] and gLite, which uses the Job Definition Language (JDL) [20]. Hence, the seamless submission of computational jobs from one client to different infrastructures can only be ensured when all technologies are compliant with the same description language such as the Job Submission and Description Language (JSDL) [24] and their specification extensions like Single Program Multiple Data (SPMD). Hence, the middleware should provide interfaces that accept jobs in this description (e.g. OGSA-BES [26]). Although the progress of JSDL is quite far the emerging amount of extensions break again the obtained interoperability in terms of job submission. To support even more complex jobs we also state the requirement for a common workflow language among the Grid middleware technologies, but research in this area reveals that this seems not to be achievable because of the huge differences in definition of complex application jobs.

The last requirement of the job management layer is related to the execution of the computational job itself. At the time of writing there is no agreement about a common execution environment that is needed when performing cross-Grid jobs that require for instance special visualization libraries or rather general message passing interface libraries. In addition, many applications make use of the environment variable provided via the Grid middleware systems in the started process at the HTC or HPC resource. Since there is no common definition available on this variable setting, jobs cannot be run on resources that provide access via a different Grid middleware system. In this context, virtual machines are not still widely adopted in production infrastructures and early analysis reveals that the performance does not satisfy end-user demands especially in HPC Grids. As a consequence, we raise the demand for the definition of an execution environment profile that has been recently started within GIN of OGF (i.e. Worker Node Profile).

3.3 Data Management

Figure 1 illustrates three major requirements at the data management layer. Starting with the lack of a common defined set of data transfer techniques, we observe that the most e-science infrastructures adopt different concepts. Many Grid infrastructures (TeraGrid, EGEE, OSG) adopt GridFTP for large data transfers while other infrastructures (e.g. DEISA) rather rely on distributed parallel file systems (e.g. IBM Global Parallel File System). While many other technologies exist such as secure FTP, ByteIO, and parallel HTTP, we raise the demand for an interface that abstracts from the different concepts and provides one standard interface for data transfer. Recently, OGF worked on the Data Movement Interface (DMI) that seems to satisfy this requirement but which is still work in progress, especially in terms of third-party credential delegation that is used, for instance, for GridFTP transfers underneath.

We also state the requirements need to explicitly define the link between job description and data transfer specifications that are required when jobs are using data staging in/out functionalities. That means all computational jobs that may even be submitted through OGSA-BES compliant interfaces and use JSDL would fail since the data staging definitions within the JSDLs are not defined and thus are implemented in proprietary ways in the Grid middlewares. More recently, work in OGF has been performed on the HPC File Staging Profile (FSB) that aligns OGSA-BES interfaces with FTP-based data transfers. However, since FTP is also not widely adopted within e-science infrastructures, we still require a more sophisticated set of profiles that support a wider variety of data transfer technologies.

Closely aligned with data transfer are data access and storage technologies such as SRM [28] implementations (e.g. DCache, Storm, Castor). That means several functions of SRM interface implementations (e.g. moveTo operation) use the underneath data transer technologies (e.g. GridFTP) to transfer the data. The same is valid for WS-DAIS [29] implementations (e.g. OGSA-DAI, or AMGA Metadata Catalog) that rely on GridFTP for the transport of large blob files when, for instance, relational databases are used. In addition to the use of SRM interface implementations in infrastructures (e.g. EGEE) and WS-DAIS interface implementations in infrastructures (e.g. NGS), several infrastructures also rely on SRB or iRods (e.g. OSG) that neither provide a SRM nor WS-DAIS interface. In order to use all these technologies transparently during cross-Grid job submissions with data staging, the listed data access technologies must provide a standard interface such as SRM or WS-DAIS. Also, we require a precise definition how these interface can be used during data staging using JSDL-compliant jobs.

More recently, we also indicated end-user requirements to support the access to digital repositories that deliver content resources such as any form of scientific data and output, including scientific/technical reports, working papers, articles and original research data. In this context, metadata is important to store/extract data conveniently. As a consequence, we require middleware that allows for the attachment/detachment of semantics to computed data on the infrastructures before any data is stored. Also, we require different services such as search, collection, profiling, or recommendation that bridge the functionality between Grid middleware and digital repositories. In this context, the DRIVER project [25] is working on a good step towards the right direction in inter-networking European scientific respositories. But the precise links between deployed job and data management technologies and digital repositories are not defined yet although required more in more in scientific use cases that use computational resources within Grids to perform efficient queries for knowledge data in repositories.

4 Related Work

As already mentioned in the introduction of this paper, the OGSA initially defined by Foster et al. [8] defines an architecture model taking many requirements from e-science and e-business into account. Our work is motivated by lessons learned from e-science infrastructure interoperability efforts that raise the demand for an interoperability reference model that is trimmed down in functionality compared to OGSA, is less complex than OGSA, and thus realistically to implement and to specify in more detail than OGSA.

Another reference model that is related is the Enterprise Grid Alliance (EGA) reference model [27]. The goal of this model is to make it easier for commercial providers to make use of Grid computing in their data centers. This model comprises three different parts: a lexicon of Grid terms, a model for classifying the management and lifecycles of Grid components, and a set of use cases demonstrating requirements for Grid computing in businesses. In contrast to our work, this reference model is rather focussed on business requirements, while we take requirements mainly from the scientific community into account.

5 Conclusion

In this paper we raised the demand for an interoperability reference model based on experiences and lessons learned from many interoperability projects. We can conclude that the requirements identified from these efforts lead to a reference model that can be seen as a trimmed down version of the OGSA in terms of functionality and complexity. The requirements defined in this paper can be used to specify the core building blocks of a realistically implementable reference model for interoperable e-science infrastructures based on experiences and lessons learned over the last years in GIN and other interoperability projects. We foresee that many building blocks of this reference model are already deployed on the infrastructures and only minor additions have to be done in order to achieve interoperable e-science infrastructures. The definition of this reference model is work in progress.

References

1. Distributed European Infrastructure for Supercomputing Applications (DEISA) http://www.deisa.eu, Cited 10 October 2008
2. Riedel, M. et al.: Interoperation of World-Wide Production e-Science Infrastructures, accepted for Concurrency and Computation: Practice and Experience Journal, (2008)
3. The Web Services Resource Framework Technical Committee http://www.oasis-open.org/committees/wsrf/, Cited 10 October 2008
4. Riedel, M. et al.: Improving e-Science with Interoperability of the e-Infrastructures EGEE and DEISA. In: Proceedings of the 31st International Convention MIPRO, Conference on Grid and Visualization Systems (GVS), Opatija, Croatia, ISBN 978-953-233-036-6, pages 225–231 (2008)
5. The Open Middleware Infrastructure Institute for Europe http://www.omii-europe.org, Cited 10 October 2008
6. Streit, A. et al.: UNICORE - From Project Results to Production Grids, Advances in Parallel omputing 14, Elsevier, 357–376 (2005)
7. EU Fusion for ITER Applications http://www.euforia-project.eu, Cited 10 October 2008
8. Foster, I. et al.: The Physiology of the Grid. In: Grid Computing - Making the Global Infrastructure a Reality, John Wiley & Sons Ltd, pages 217–249 (2002)
9. Wide In Silico Docking on Malaria Project http://wisdom.eu-egee.fr, Cited 10 October 2008
10. Riedel, M. et al.: Classification of Different Approaches for e-Science Applications in Next Generation Computing Infrastructures. Accepted for publication in: Proceedings of the e-science Conference, Indianapolis, Indiana, USA (2008)
11. Wide In Silico Docking on Malaria Project http://www.euindiagrid.org/ , Cited 10 October 2008
12. Gudgin, M. et al.: SOAP Version 1.2 Part 1: Messaging Framework, W3C Rec. (2003)
13. WS-Interoperability (WS-I) http://www.ws-i.org , Cited 10 October 2008
14. Box, D. et al.:WS-Addressing (WS-A), W3C Member Submission. (2004)
15. Amazons Elastic Computing Cloud (EC2) http://aws.amazon.com/ec2, Cited 10 October 2008
16. Venturi, V. et al.: Using SAML-based VOMS for Authorization within Web Services-based UNICORE Grids, In:Proceedings of 3rd UNICORE Summit 2007 in Springer LNCS 4854, Euro-Par 2007 Workshops: Parallel Processing, pages 112–120 (2007)
17. Enabling Grids for e-Science Project http://public.eu-egee.org, Cited 10 October 2008
18. Alfieri, R. et al.: From gridmapfile to voms: managing authorization in a grid environment, In: Future Generation Comp. Syst., 21(4):, pages 549–558 (2005)
19. Open Science Grid (OSG) http://www.opensciencegrid.org, Cited 10 October 2008
20. Laure, E. et al.: Programming The Grid with gLite, Computational Methods in Science and Technology, Scientific Publishers OWN, 33–46 (2006)
21. TeraGrid http://www.teragrid.org, Cited 10 October 2008
22. Foster, I. et al.: Globus Toolkit version 4: Software for Service-Oriented Science, In: Proceedings of IFIP International Conference on Network and Parallel Computing, LNCS 3779, pages 213–223 (2005)
23. NorduGrid http://www.nordugrid.org/ , Cited 10 October 2008
24. Anjomshoaa, A. et al.: Job Submission Description Language (JSDL) Specification, Version 1.0, OGF GFD 136
25. DRIVER Project http://www.driver-repository.eu , Cited 10 October 2008
26. Foster, I. et al.: OGSA - Basic Execution Services, OGF GFD 108
27. EGA Reference Model http://www.ogf.org/documents/06322r00EGA RefMod-Reference-Model.pdf, Cited 10 October 2008

28. Sim, A. et al.: Storage Resource Manager Interface Specification Version 2.2, OGF GFD 129
29. Antonioletti, M. et al.: Web Services Data Access and Integration - The Core (WS-DAI) Specification, Version 1.0, OGF GFD 74

Interactive Scientific Visualization of High-resolution Brain Imagery Over Networked Tiled Display

SeokHo Son[1], JunHee Hong[2], ChangHyeok Bae[1], Sung Chan Jun[2], and JongWon Kim[1]

Networked Media Lab., Gwangju Institute of Science and Technology (GIST), South Korea [1]

{shson, chbae, jongwon}@nm.gist.ac.kr

Bio-Computing Lab., Gwangju Institute of Science and Technology (GIST), South Korea [2]

{jun0476, scjun}@gist.ac.kr

Abstract In this paper, we discuss our on-going efforts for an interactive scientific visualization of high-resolution brain imagery over networked tiled display. It targets to visualize a brain in both 2D and 3D. It also supports multiple high-resolution displays of brain images by integrating networked tiled display while providing interactive control of display resolution and view direction. In order to construct an appropriate visualization system for brain imaging researches, we study and compare existing visualization systems using a networked tiled display. Based on this comparison, we integrate visualization features on our brain visualization system. Finally, to verify the usefulness of the proposed approach, an initial implementation of EIT brain image visualization is being made.

1 Introduction

For collaborative types of next-generation scientific researches, often referred as e-Science, new sets of cyber infrastructures are expected to be built with the support of ubiquitous IT technologies. Current development of e-Science infrastructure is largely influenced by high-performance network-supported grid computing. That is, collaborative research environments established through the grid computing and follow-ups are now providing the basic infrastructure for e-Science. For scientific collaboration, it is required to support the advanced level of collaborative visual sharing among knowledge workers distributed geographically [1]. However, traditional room-based collaboration environments can only provide limited display resolution, uncomfortable sharing of visuals and documents,

O.-H. Byeon et al. (eds.), *Future Application and Middleware Technology on e-Science*,
DOI 10.1007/978-1-4419-1719-5_13,

difficult operation of collaboration tools. To solve these restrictions, based on the ultra-high-resolution networked tiled displays, prototype collaboration environments are being developed to realize practical and interactive collaboration of science researchers. The networked tiled display enables collaborators to employ a tiled set of display devices as one virtual high-resolution display device by connecting them through a high-speed network. It can seamlessly present high-resolution visual data with interactive display commands (e.g., show, hide, resize, and move). Also, it can simultaneously visualize multiple display instances on top of clustered display tiles. For example, a networked tiled display named as HiperWall [2] is composed of 50 tiles connected through a 10G network and provides total 204,800,000-pixel display resolution.

With this research infrastructure of networked tiled display, we consider integrating networked tiled display system with scientific visualization area. Scientific visualization translates data into visual images in order to support people to analyze and verify scientific data in an intuitive manner. To realize scientific visualization employing networked tiled display, as an example trial, we first investigate the scientific visualization of brain imaging. Recently brain imaging has been paid far great attention since several new brain imaging techniques have been developed. It now provides clinicians and neuroscientists with more detailed information on brain structure and brain functionality. Among the existing brain imaging visualization efforts, we particularly investigate EIT (Electrical Impedance Tomography) and EEG (Electroencephalography) brain imaging techniques.

Accordingly, in this paper, we discuss our on-going efforts for an interactive scientific visualization of high-resolution brain imagery over networked tiled display. It targets to visualize EIT brain images in both 2D and 3D. It also supports multiple high-resolution brain images by integrating networked tiled display while providing interactive control of display resolution and view direction. Note that, to provide this type of high-performance scientific visualization, it is highly required to consider performance problems related to computation, graphic rendering, and display. Thus, in our current trial, we are trying to integrate the effective features of existing visualization schemes over networked tiled display approaches.

2 Brain visualization and visualization systems

Here, we introduce brain visualizations as an example of scientific visualization, and visualization systems with networked tiled display. We initially investigate the scientific visualization of brain imaging. Among the existing brain imaging visualization efforts, we particularly investigate EIT and EEG brain imaging techniques.

2-1 Brain visualization

2-1-1 Current brain imagings and their visualization

2-1-1-1 MEG (Magnetoencelphlography) and EEG (Electroencephalography)

MEG and EEG are used to image electrical activity in the brain. Clusters of thousands of synchronously activated pyramidal cortical neurons are the main generators of MEG and EEG signals. MEG is an imaging technique used to measure the magnetic fields produced by electrical activity in the brain via extremely sensitive devices such as superconducting quantum interference devices. EEG is one of the perfectly non-invasive brain imaging tools and it supports higher temporal resolution up to a fraction of millisecond, thereby being very useful for brain dynamics. EEG detects the electrical potential generated by direct electric activity in the brain and it can image brain activities.

2-1-1-2 EIT (Electrical Impedance Tomography)

EIT is a tool to estimate and to visualize the distribution of electrical conductivity of human brain. Weak currents are input through one pair of electrodes, and the induced electric potential distributions are measured through remaining electrodes. EIT is especially good at monitoring lung function, detecting breast cancer and a brain tumor. Also, EIT is better than other brain imaging techniques by its mobility and low cost. But, EIT demands algorithm which images the conductivity like MEG/EEG techniques. Particularly we have to solve ellipse equation of the head. As an increase the spatial resolution of the head, we have to solve the large-scale linear system. EIT technique is in initial stage of development. So, research of EIT imaging technique is not sufficient yet.

2-1-2 Current brain visualization tools

We introduce three brain visualization tools (MRIVIEW, BrainStorm, and EIDORS). MRIVIEW is a tool providing readability of raw MRI data, MRI display in 2D/3D, and combination display of anatomical and functional information. Brain Storm is the tool visualizing MEG/EEG signal on MRI image. Lastly, EIDORS is a tool to calculate EIT as well as visualize EIT images in 2D/3D.

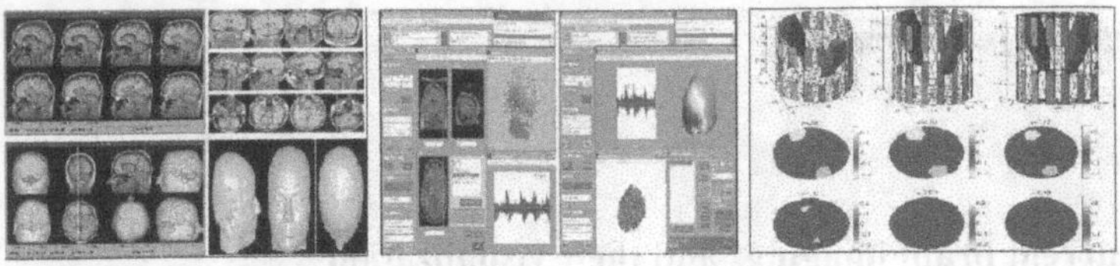

Fig. 1. Current brain visualization tools

Fig. 1 shows tools shapes of MRIVIEW, BrainStorm, and EIDORS respectively. These tools usually display multiple images to give much information to the user. However, these tools are not enough to display multiple brain images in high resolution. We expect users desire to use an infrastructure making them intuitively watch multiple and high resolution brain contents in one large display.

2-2 Visualization systems using a networked tiled display

To construct an appropriate visualization system for brain imaging researches, we study and compare existing visualization systems. Based on classification and comparison of existing visualization system, we consider integrating visualization features on our brain visualization system.

2-2-1 Existing visualization systems

As of now, to drive networked tiled display, a number of display middlewares are developed including SAGE (scalable and adaptive graphics environment) [3] and CGLX (cross-platform cluster graphic library) [4].

SAGE is highly linked with visualization-oriented display applications such as JuxtaView, Vol-a-Tile, Raintable. JuxtaView [5] supports the shared visualization, based on distributed memory, of large-size images by sharing whole image with a visualization cluster. Vol-a-Tile [6] provides OpenGL-based graphic visualization by boosting rendering speed with parallel rendering. Raintable [7] interactively combines both image and graphic display to show dynamic change of rain flows over mountain areas. RainTable uses pre-computation concept to handle large set of data to be displayed. Finally, OpenGL-friendly CGLX provides an easy-to-use framework to interface OpenGL-based visualization programs with tiled-display-integrated clusters.

2-2-2 The comparison of visualization systems

In order to display high resolution graphics on networked tiled display, data distribution strategy has to be determined for system design related to computation, graphic rendering, and display.

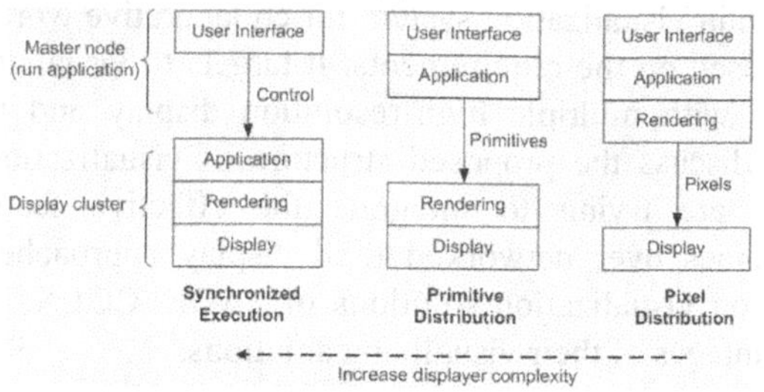

Fig. 2. Data distribution strategy on networked tiled display

Fig. 2 describes three different approaches of data distribution strategy: control, primitives, or pixels distribution [8]. In case of control distribution, a copy of the application runs on each display nodes. The master node just handles user-interface events, and sends control information. In case of primitive distribution, the application is running on the master node. The application sends graphics primitives over the network to the display cluster which renders and displays them. To each display machines, the rendering load is assigned. In case of pixels distribution, structure of visualization system becomes simple because each display requires only display pixels. So, processing and storage needs of display cluster are simplified. However, resolution of the image is limited by network bandwidth.

Existing visualization systems can be classified according to data distribution strategy between master node and display cluster. Raintable and JuxtaView are classified as synchronized execution. So, they require better hardware set of display cluster. Also, it is hard for the synchronized execution to share their views with multiparty users in a different place. In contrast, they can show high speed display. Vol-a-tile and CGLX are classified as primitive distribution (i.e. OpenGL context distribution for OpenGL application). In those cases, they require display cluster which have better graphic hardware to render OpenGL context again. However, display resolution is not limited by network bandwidth. Finally, SAGE is classified as pixel distribution. It shows simple structure and simple display cluster. It is easy for SAGE to share their views with remote site. Also, SAGE can support multiple displays of several images on a networked tiled display.

3 Design of the proposed brain visualization system over networked tiled display

Here, we discuss our on-going efforts for an interactive scientific visualization of high resolution brain imagery over networked tiled display. First, we consider requirements of brain visualization system for collaborative works, and we set the system features based on the requirements. It targets to visualize brain images in both 2D and 3D with multiple high-resolution display and user interactions. Furthermore, we discuss the proposed structure of visualization system. In our current trial, we are trying to integrate the effective features of existing visualization schemes over networked tiled display approaches. The proposed structure focuses on visualization solutions of SAGE, CGLX, and RainTable in order to take advantages of their visualizing solutions.

3-1 System features and requirements

We introduce features of the proposed brain visualization system in this section. The objective of this system is to support scientific collaboration of brain images. Therefore, the proposed visualization considers which contents have to be displayed and which interactions have to be supported for brain researchers.

In the proposed visualization system, there are three brain contents (i.e. 3D brain mesh, MRI image, EIT image) which show shape of a brain and its functionalities. The brain contents are large scale and high resolution images, and those multiple contents are displayed on one large display device.

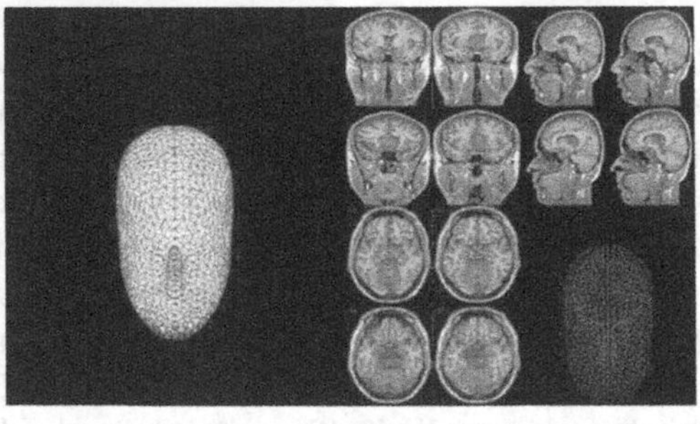

Fig. 3. The brain contents in the proposed brain visualization system

Fig. 3 illustrates brain contents which the proposed visualization system displays. It is composed of the 3d brain mesh, MRI images, and EIT images. The image on the left side of the Fig. 3 is 3d brain mesh which show entire shape of brain in 3D. The set of images on the right side of the Fig. 3 are MRI images of sagittal axis, coronal axis, and axial axis. MRI images are overlaid with EIT images.

There are three main interactions to help collaborative brain researches in this brain visualization system. The first interaction is the image selection. This interaction let user watch set of MRI/EIT images. User can select those images by pointing an anomaly position on 3d brain mesh. Then, the system displays MRI/EIT matched on brain position. The second interaction is the control of 3d brain mesh. The brain visualization system supports a control interaction for 3d brain. With this interaction user can control resolution of 3d brain, position and rotation of 3d brain. The other interaction is the image scale control where user can freely enlarge size of images displayed on tiled-display. Therefore, user can easily focus on a MRI or an EIT image which user want to see details.

In order to satisfy system features, this brain visualization system has to support the high resolution display of contents, multiple image display, interaction between brain contents, and the real time interaction. Thus, in the next section, we explain the proposed visualization structure which satisfies the system requirements.

3-2 Structure of the brain visualization system

In order to make the brain visualization system satisfies visualization requirements, we propose structure of the brain visualization system which integrates several features of other visualization solutions. The proposed structure focuses on visualization solutions of SAGE, CGLX, and RainTable in order to take advantages of their visualizing solutions.

The proposed system uses data distribution concepts of SAGE and CGLX to provide high resolution display and multiple image display. SAGE uses pixel distribution strategy, and CGLX uses OpenGL context distribution strategy. The pixel distribution strategy lets networked tiled display easily show and control multiple images. It is easy to display images composed of pixels with SAGE. Alternatively, the resolution of images to be displayed is limited by network bandwidth between a master node and a display cluster. On the other hand, resolution of graphics in CGLX is not limited by network bandwidth because CGLX does not distribute pixels of the image to the display cluster in order to display. The CGLX master node running graphic application captures OpenGL contexts and distributes OpenGL contexts having fewer amounts of data. Finally, each display nodes in the display cluster render OpenGL contexts again in order to generate pixels. Therefore, resolution of graphics is not limited by network bandwidth generally. However, CGLX can display only one OpenGL application at a time on tiled display. So, it is not suitable for the multiple images display. Without the feature of multiple display images, it is hard for brain visualization system to support interactions controlling each multiple images.

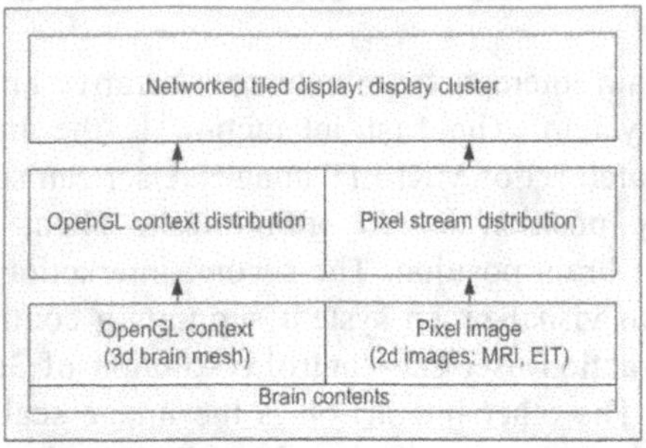

Fig. 4. The visualization structure of the proposed system

Fig. 4 describes the proposed visualizing structure of media distribution strategy to display brain contents over networked tiled display. In this structure, OpenGL context which is the 3d brain mesh is displayed with OpenGL context distribution, and pixel images of the MRI/EIT are displayed with the pixel stream distribution. By using both pixel distribution strategy of SAGE and OpenGL contexts distribution strategy of CGLX, the proposed system can support both high resolution display and multiple image display.

In order to increase interaction speed, the proposed system takes the advantage of the pre-computation concept from RainTable. When a user selects an anomaly location on 3d brain mesh, a matched set of MRI images and EIT images have to be displayed. However, visualizing EIT requires long time to be generated. It is hard to get EIT images in real time because EIT algorithm demands very long time for calculation generally. So, in order to increase interaction speed, the system calculates and generates whole EIT images in advance. With this pre-computation scheme, the proposed brain visualization system can display set of pre-computed EIT images matched with the anomaly location on a tiled-display immediately after a user selects an anomaly location.

4 Initial implementation of the proposed visualization system

In this chapter, we discuss about actual implementation for initial version of the proposed system. Also, implementation results in the real environment are shown with photographs.

4-1 The structure of the implemented system4-1 The structure of the implemented system

In this section, we show initial implementation of the proposed visualization system. This initial implementation include basic system feature except OpenGL context distribution part. The implemented system is based on SAGE structure because SAGE already provides various functions for the networked tiled display.

Fig. 5 shows the overall structure of the implemented system. We can see how brain contents are displayed over networked tiled displays. The master node generates brain contents, and brain contents are converted into pixel streams. This pixel streams are sent to display cluster, and brain contents are displayed. Meanwhile interactions are supported by a mouse and a keyboard. By the mouse, the user can select anomaly location to see designated MRI/EIT images. Also, the user can control the 3d brain mesh. Using keyboard, the user can enlarge MRI/EIT images.

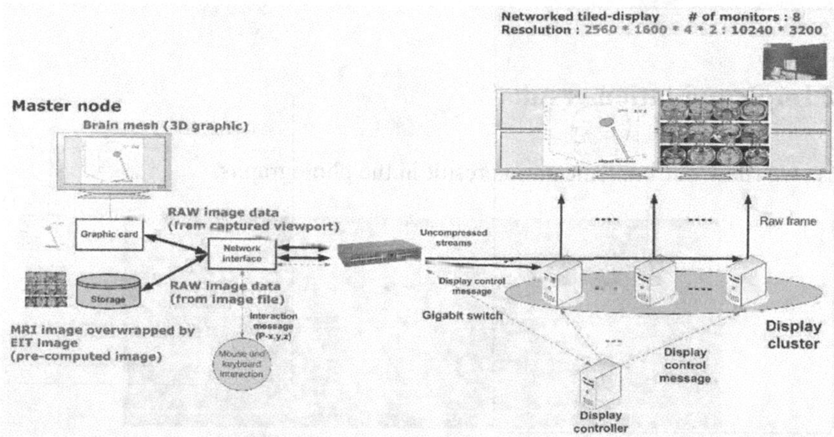

Fig. 5. Implementation structure of initial version of the proposed visualization system

In order to implement the system structure, we separate the pixel generation methods for separated controls of brain contents. Usually, SAGE captures the frame buffer rasterized from OpenGL application to generate pixel streams. However, it is not appropriate for multiple images display which enables separated control of brain images because captured pixels are considered as one application on the tiled-display. If the both 3d context and 2d images are captured together, it is hard for the user to control brain contents separately. Furthermore, resolution of images is limited by the frame buffer size specified in graphic card. Therefore, the system differentiates pixel generation methods before the system distributes pixel streams to the display cluster. By differentiating pixel generation methods by the capturing frame buffer and the opening image files, the system can display larger size of the contents resolution and support controls on separated contents.

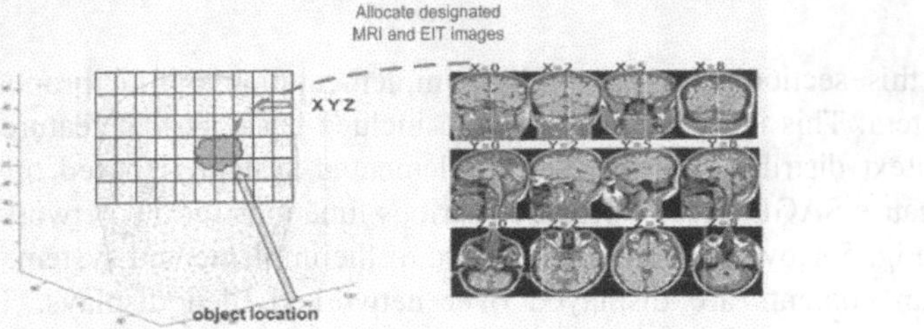

Fig. 6. Implementation of the pre-computation

Fig. 6 shows implementation of the pre-computation. The proposed system makes grid sections on 3d brain mesh. And so, the system generates EIT images in advance. These EIT images are attached on each matched MRI images. Finally, MRI images with EIT are designated on the grid sections of 3d brain mesh.

4-2 Implementation results

Here, we show our implementation result in the photographs.

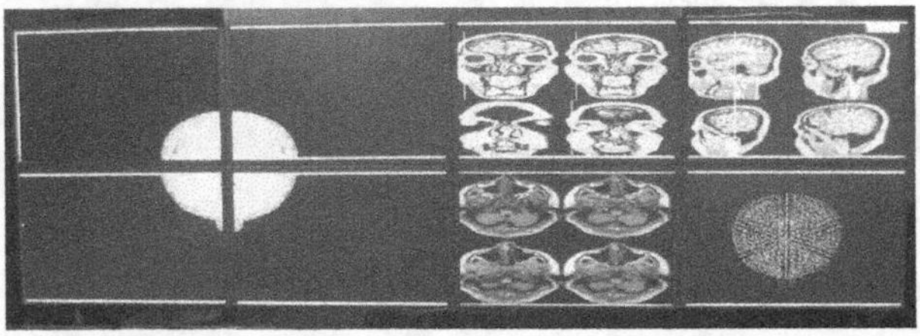

Fig. 7. Implementation result of initial version of the proposed visualization system (overall)

Fig. 7 shows the implementation result of the initial version of the proposed interactive brain visualization system. As we can see in Fig, brain contents are displayed on networked tiled display composed of 8 display devices. Total resolution of this tiled display is 10240 pixels multiplied by 3200 pixels. In this system, we can easily watch large scale of brain contents.

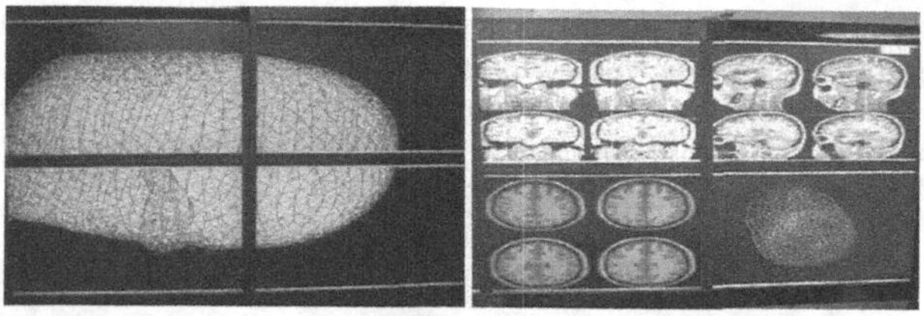

Fig. 8. Implementation result (3d brain mesh and MRI/EIT images)

Fig. 8 shows the interactions of the implemented system. Fig. 8 shows 3d brain mesh is manipulated by the user. Also, it shows sliced MRI images by sagittal axis, coronal axis, and axial axis. We can see red color on MRI images. It shows EIT data matched on selected anomaly location on 3d brain by the user. In conclusion, with the proposed system, researchers and collaborators can easily control brain contents and they can focus on their interest.

5 Conclusion and future works

In this paper, we discussed our on-going efforts for an interactive scientific visualization of high-resolution brain imagery over networked tiled display. It targets to visualize brain images in both 2D/3D with multiple high-resolution display and user interactions. In our current trial, we are trying to integrate the effective features of existing visualization schemes. By using both pixel distribution strategy and OpenGL contexts distribution strategy, the system can support both high resolution display and multiple image display. Also, pre-computation of EIT images are considered to increase interaction speed. Finally, in order to verify usefulness of the system, we implemented initial version of the proposed visualization system. The next steps of our works are completing implementation and modeling of a visualization system to evaluate performance of the proposed system.

Reference

1 B Corrie et. al., "Towards quality of experience in advanced collaborative environments," *in Proc. Workshop on Advanced Collaborative Environments*, Seattle, June 2003.
2 HiperWall: http://hiperwall.calit2.uci.edu/.
3 L Renambot et. al., "SAGE: The scalable adaptive graphics environment," *in Proc. Workshop on Advanced Collaborative Environments*, Nice, France, Sep. 2004.
4 CGLX Project: http://vis.ucsd.edu/~cglx/.
5 N K Krishnaprasad et. al., "JuxtaView – a tool for interactive visualization of large imagery on scalable tiled displays," in *Proc. IEEE Cluster 2004*, San Diego, Sep. 2004.

6 N Schwarz et. al., "Vol-a-Tile - a tool for interactive exploration of large volumetric data on scalable tiled displays," in *Proc. IEEE Visualization 2004*, Austin, Oct. 2004.
7 Rain Table: http://www.evl.uic.edu/cavern/mc/raintable/.
8 H Chen et. al., "Data distribution strategies for high-resolution displays", Computers & Graphics, Volume 25, Issue 5, Pages 811-818, Oct. 2001

Object-Oriented Implementation of the Finite-Difference Time-Domain Method in Parallel Computing Environment

Kyungwon Chun, Huioon Kim, Hyunpyo Hong, and Youngjoo Chung

Department of Information and Communications, School of Photon Science and Technology, 261 Cheomdan-gwagiro, Buk-gu, Gwangju 500-712 Republic of Korea

E-mail: {kwchun, pcandme, realhhp, ychung}@gist.ac.kr

Abstract: GMES which stands for GIST Maxwell's Equations Solver is a Python package for a Finite-Difference Time-Domain (FDTD) simulation. The FDTD method widely used for electromagnetic simulations is an algorithm to solve the Maxwell's equations. GMES follows Object-Oriented Programming (OOP) paradigm for the good maintainability and usability. With the several optimization techniques along with parallel computing environment, we could make the fast and interactive implementation. Execution speed has been tested in a single host and Beowulf class cluster. GMES is open source and available on the web (http://www.sf.net/projects/gmes).

PACS: 02.70.-c

Keywords: Finite-Difference Time-Domain, Object Oriented Programming, Python, Parallel Computing, MPI, GMES

1. Introduction

The FDTD method is widely used for the computational electromagnetic simulations [1]. The FDTD method leads to time- and space-domain solutions of the difference equations converted from the differential form of the Maxwell's equations. Though the spatial discretization property causes long simulation time and large computational domain requirement, the versatile and intuitive properties of FDTD give rise to be that many commercial or non-commercial simulation software implements the FDTD method. These programs deal with applications of range from near-DC to optical-frequency, and scale from several nanometers to planet-wide.

O.-H. Byeon et al. (eds.), *Future Application and Middleware Technology on e-Science*, DOI 10.1007/978-1-4419-1719-5_14, © Springer Science+Business Media, LLC 2010

Many researchers develop their own FDTD programs which satisfies their specific needs. Typically simulation program developers try to acquire fast calculation speed and small computational domain requirement, particularly for FDTD developers. Usually, these attitudes tend to obstacle usable and maintainable design of the implementation. However, if we consider the scientific exactitude of the simulation program or unexpected design change as the research progress in the future, the maintainable design is, in that sense, a valuable design principle.

Object Oriented Programming (OOP) paradigm provides the way to a maintainable design. The problems, vast number of entangled parameters in complex algorithm, an unexpected change of design with respect to research progress, are the familiar issues to the researchers in computer engineering field. Computer engineers have solved these problems using OOP paradigm. All data in the program have corresponding self-sufficient modules, and we can concentrate on each module, not a whole bunch of code. When an unexpected design change happens, we struggle just with a few specific modules. Thus, the development period and maintenance cost can be reduced.

GMES was designed to have good maintainability and usability. All the development decisions, from the data structure design to choice of a programming language follow this design goal. Of course, this design goal brings out significant problem which is low execution speed. We had solved this problem in various ways. Some experiences to overcome this problem will be described.

2. Implementation

2.1 Python

Python is an interpreted programming language which supports multi-paradigm such as OOP, structured programming, and functional programming. Clear and simple syntax of Python makes it possible to develop a usable and maintainable program in a short period of time [2]. Python plays the role of a main programming language in GMES. GMES heavily depends on Python for memory management, error handling, input/output, and user interaction. All data types are based on the Python built-in types and ndarray of NumPy [3]. Just few part of code which has a significant influence on the iteration speed has been implemented in C++.

GMES has a form of a Python package and all data types are provided as classes. A user can make a new data type by inheriting an existing one or implementing the Abstract Base Class (ABC). Also, you can give a new feature to GMES for your own need. These kinds of jobs can be done in Python environment only. Both ways of batch style script or interactive environment provided by Python interpreter are supported. Though GMES is blessed with a lot of the convenient features of Python, the relatively low speed of the interpreted programming languages slows down the execution speed of GMES. As Python became popular in numerical calculation area, various ways to overcome this drawback was contrived. GMES uses some of these methods for speed-up.

2.2 Design

A three-dimensional space lattice of GMES is comprised of a multiplicity of Yee cells, as shown in Fig. 1. Each field component in Yee lattice has a corresponding value of material parameters representing electric or magnetic material properties. In classical FDTD design, these material properties are stored in a separate contiguous memory, to save the memory space and acquire fast access to the value [1]. In this manner, the addition of new material types affects other part of the program. Also, it is difficult to use totally different type of material in the same execution of simulation. Instead of it, the each field component of each point in Yee cell can have a corresponding object which contains the update algorithm to calculate the electric or magnetic field interaction and necessary material properties. We named the Abstract Base Class (ABC) for this object as Pointwise Material, because the derived concrete class will be assigned to each point of Yee lattice.

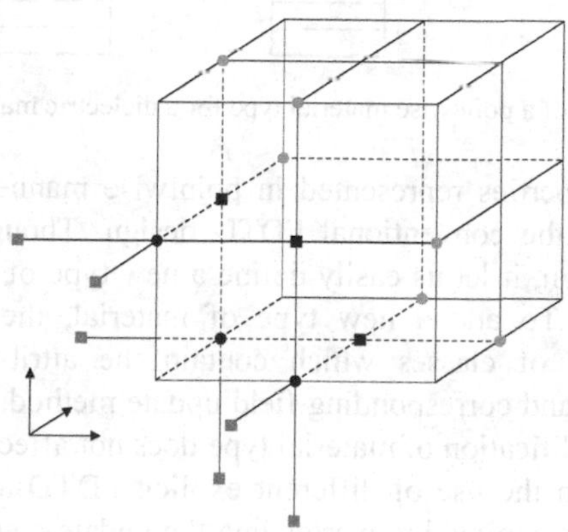

Fig. 1. Yee lattice in 3-dimension for a single grid voxel. The blue and red points are the buffers for the synchronization in parallel environment.

The base class of PointwiseMaterial in Fig. 2 has a virtual method for the field update algorithm. The leaf classes classified by the electromagnetic field component define the virtual method of the parent class. This way of dynamic binding makes the code simple, because the use of PointwiseMaterial objects eliminates the conditional statements in codes. Also, defining the leaf classes in component-wise manner keeps each leaf class small, by removing unnecessary attributes. Each object contains only the required material properties to update the electric or magnetic field at that point. This design decouples the material data from the other material data on the other area. Thus, arbitrary combination of different type of materials can be used in a single simulation. Though the electromagnetic field values are required during the field update procedure, the field values are stored at separate contiguous array. There are three reasons for that. Firstly, the electromagnetic field is not tightly bound to the material property. Secondly, the update procedure requires field values on neighbor points. Thirdly, by using contiguous memory, synchronization on parallel environment will work faster.

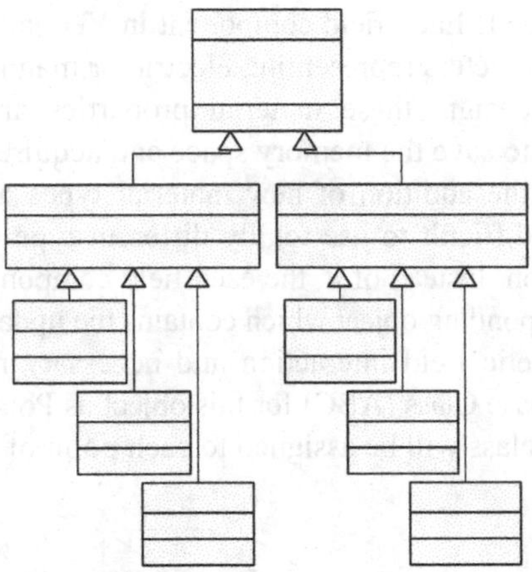

Fig. 2. A UML diagram of a pointwise material type for a dielectric material

The material properties represented in pointwise manner, generally consume more memory than the conventional FDTD design. Though this is the biggest problem of our design, it let us easily define a new type of material, not only the arbitrary use of it. To add a new type of material, the only thing to do is implementing a set of classes which contain the attributes representing the material properties, and corresponding field update method, in the form of Fig. 2. This addition or modification of material type does not affect the other parts of the program at all. Even the use of different explicit FDTD algorithm, like higher-order method, can be applied by overloading the update method. Though all these things can be implemented with nothing more than the Python language, if faster speed is required, the pointwise-material-derived classes can be written in a compiled language. The specific example and the performance increase will be shown later.

2.3 Speed Optimization

As mentioned earlier, the execution speed of interpreted programming language is slower than the compiled language. There are several ways to speed up our Python program. The easiest one to try is Psyco which generates the improved machine code in run-time. By adding just a few lines of code, we can expect speed-up of several times [4]. The second one to try is Pyrex, a Python-like language with C data types. It allows us writing a code, much more Python-like but with the performance of C [5]. The last one we tried is extending Python with C++ language. This method is traditional compared to the previous two approaches but gives us the best result in general. The Simplified Wrapper and Interface Generator (SWIG) saves our times to write a bunch of interfacing codes [6].

To check the execution speed enhancement, we prepared a simple 2-dimensional *transverse-magnetic mode with respect to z* (TM_z) mode FDTD application using GMES. As you can see in Fig. 3, this application simulates cylindrical electromagnetic field in the air. When we executed this application with 180x180x1 Yee cells at Pentium 4 2.6 GHz Debian GNU/Linux machine, it took 394 seconds for 100 iterations on the average. We tested the optimization variants with different number of iterations. The results are shown in Fig. 4. The version using Psyco and Pyrex showed about 1.4 and 1.6 times speed-ups, respectively. In the optimization using Pyrex, PointwiseMaterial and derived classes were implemented in Pyrex. When we implemented PointwiseMaterial class family in C++, it showed 3.7 times speed-up compared to the Python only version. The extended Python version with the machine code optimization using Psyco showed 8.7 times speed-up, as can be seen in Fig. 4.

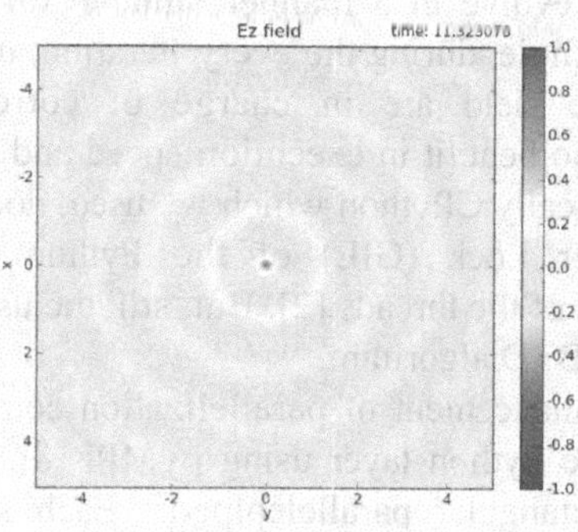

Fig. 3. The visualization of the 2 dimensional FDTD benchmark program. This figure was generated by the GMES on-time display features which use Matplotlib [7].

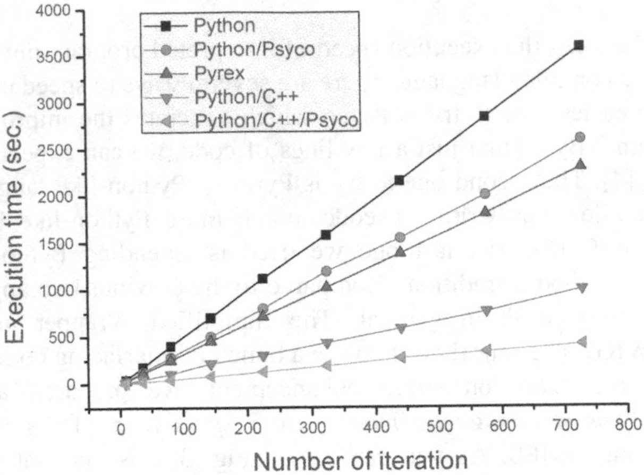

Fig. 4. The execution speed test results of our various optimizations

2.4 Parallelization

The FDTD algorithm has a good structure to apply the parallel calculation using a thread and Massive Passing Interface (MPI). The x, y, and z components of electromagnetic fields evolve in a manner suitable to simultaneous calculation using a thread. For example, during the every iteration, update procedures of each component of electric field are in charge of corresponding threads. This implementation gives no benefit in execution speed and even degrades the speed, because Python, specifically CPython which we used, does not support full thread. The Global Interpreter Lock (GIL) of the Python interpreter prevents the simultaneous execution of the threads [2]. But, still the use of thread makes it clear the correlation of the FDTD algorithm.

The performance enhancement of parallelization comes from the use of MPI. MPI was applied in the Python layer using pyMPI [8]. The space lattice can be divided into small rectangular parallelepipeds. Each space lattice fragment is initialized and handled by separate processes. During the field update iterations, before calculation of each field update procedure, the field values on the boundary should be transferred between adjacent processes. This synchronization procedure slows down the iteration speed. So we need to adjust the node deployment in the calculation domain to minimize the amount of communication. Usually if we divide the space similar to a cube, we can get the best efficiency.

The performance enhancement by the use of MPI was tested using a 3 dimensional FDTD script which simulates the photonic crystals slab waveguide shown in Fig. 5. The whole space lattice is comprised of 376x376x24 Yee cells. Pentium 4 3.0 GHz Debian GNU/Linux clusters were used for the benchmark. We checked the initialization time and execution time of 300 iterations. The initialization procedure does not require communications between calculation processes, but the iteration procedure does. The rate of change with respect to increase of number of nodes is similar between two cases as shown in Fig. 6.

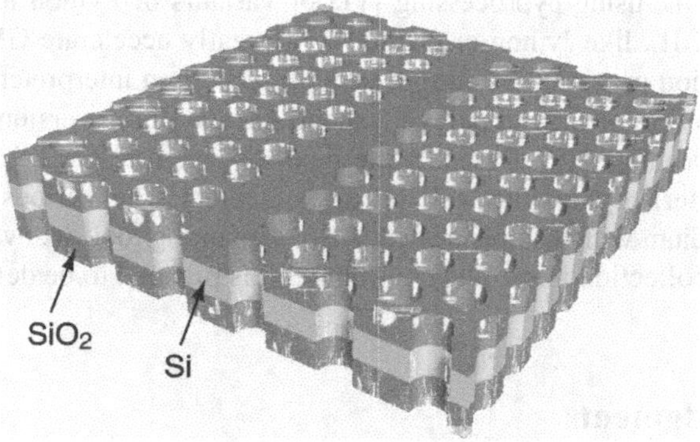

Fig. 5. A benchmark structure of a photonic crystal slab waveguide [9]

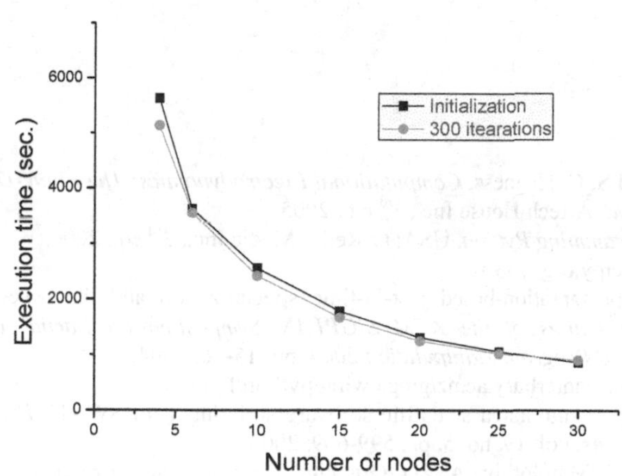

Fig. 6. Execution times of the GMES on the computing clusters

3. Conclusions and future work

We made a maintainable and productive implementation of the FDTD method, with the help of OOP and Python. GMES was design to simulate the electromagnetic field interaction with arbitrary materials and structures. The vulnerable point of speed is greatly reduced by Python extension using C++, machine code optimization, and parallel execution using MPI. But, still there is a room for further optimization. The recent version of MPI for Python, an alternate Python interface to MPI supports direct communication of memory buffers [10]. The feature will enhance the synchronization efficiency up to the C or FORTRAN version of MPI, because it eliminates the serialization overhead of a message. Evasion of GIL, using pyprocessing [11] or variants of Python interpreter which do not have GIL, like Jython or Cython will greatly accelerate GMES, especially the initialization process. The current version of Python interpreter is on the fringe on parallel environment with parallel execution. The future version of IPython will address this problem [12]. Based on the flexible design of GMES, various electromagnetic material properties will be implemented. The various dispersion and nonlinear medium will be implemented. Also, supporting tools like various launching source, data collection in parallel environment, is planned to be developed.

Acknowledgments

This research was supported by the MKE (Ministry of Knowledge Economy), Korea, under the ITRC (Information Technology Research Center) support program supervised by the IITA (Institute of Information Technology Advancement). (IITA-2008-C1090-0801-0014)

References

[1] A. Taflove and S. C. Hagness, *Computational Electrodynamics: The Finite-Difference Time-Domain Method,* Artech House Inc., 3rd ed., 2005.
[2] M. Lutz, *Programming Python*, USA: O'Reilly Media Inc., 3rd ed., 2006.
[3] http://numpy.scipy.org
[4] A. Rigo, "Representation-based just-in-time specialization and the psyco prototype for Python," *Proceedings of the ACM SIGPLAN Symposium on Partial Evaluation and Semantics-Based Program Manipulation 2004*, pp. 15-26, 2004.
[5] http://www.cosc.canterbury.ac.nz/greg.ewing/python/Pyrex
[6] D. M. Beazley, "Automated scientific software scripting with SWIG," *Future Generation Computer Systems*, vol. 19, no. 5, pp. 599-609, 2003.
[7] J. D. Hunter, "Matplotlib: A 2D Graphics Environment," *Computing in Science & Engineering*, vol. 9, no. 3, pp. 90-95, 2007.
[8] http://pympi.sourceforge.net/

[9] N. Moll and G.-L. Bona, "Comparison of three-dimensional photonic crystal slab waveguides with two-dimensional photonic crystal waveguides: Efficient butt coupling into these photonic crystal waveguides," *J. Appl. Phys.*, vol. 93, no. 9, pp. 4986-4991, 2003.
[10] L. Dalcín, R. Paz, M. Storti, and J. D'Elía, "MPI for Python: Performance improvements and MPI-2 extensions," *J. Parallel Distrib. Comput.*, vol. 68, no. 5, pp. 655-662, 2008.
[11] http://pyprocessing.berlios.de/
[12] F. Pérez and B. E. Granger, "IPython: A system for interactive scientific computing," *Comput. Sci. Eng.*, vol. 9, no. 3, 4160251, 2007.

Study on Collaborative Object Manipulation in Virtual Environment

Maria Niken Mayangsari[1], Kwon Yong-Moo[1]

[1] 39-1 Hawolgok-dong, Sungbuk-ku Imaging Media Research Center
Korea Institute of Science and Technology Seoul, 136-791, KOREA
maria.niken@imrc.kist.re.kr, ymk@kist.re.kr

Abstract. This paper presents comparative study on network collaboration performance in different immersion. Especially, the relationship between user collaboration performance and degree of immersion provided by the system is addressed and compared based on several experiments. The user tests on our system include several cases: 1) Comparison between non-haptics and haptics collaborative interaction over LAN, 2) Comparison between non-haptics and haptics collaborative interaction over Internet, and 3) Analysis of collaborative interaction between non-immersive and immersive display environments.

Keywords: Network collaboration, Immersive environment, Haptic interaction.

1 Introduction

In Collaborative Virtual Environment (CVE), multiple users can work together by interacting with the virtual objects in the VE. Several researches have been done on collaboration interaction techniques between users in CVE. Margery et al. [1] defined three levels of collaboration cases. Level 1 is where users can feel each other's presence in the VE, e.g. by representation of avatars such as performed by NICE Project [2]. Collaboration level 2 is where users can manipulate scene constraints individually. Collaboration level 3 is where users manipulate the same object together. Another classification of collaboration is by Wolff et al. [3] where they divided collaboration on same object into sequential and concurrent manipulations. The concurrent manipulation consists of manipulation of distinct and same object's attributes.

Collaboration on the same object has been focused by other research [4], where collaboration tasks are classified into symmetric and asymmetric manipulation of objects. Asymmetric manipulation is where users manipulate a virtual object by

O.-H. Byeon et al. (eds.), *Future Application and Middleware Technology on e-Science*,
DOI 10.1007/978-1-4419-1719-5_15, © Springer Science+Business Media, LLC 2010

substantially different actions, while symmetric manipulation is where users should manipulate in exactly the same way for the object to react or move.

In this research, we built an application called Virtual Dollhouse. In Virtual Dollhouse, collaboration cases are identified as two types: 1) combined inputs handling or same attribute manipulation, and 2) independent inputs handling or distinct attribute manipulation. For the first case, we use a symmetric manipulation model where the option is using common component of users' actions in order to produce the object's reactions or movements. According to Wolff et al. [3] where events traffic during object manipulations is studied, the manipulation on the same object's attribute generated the most events. Thus, we can focus our study on manipulation on the same object's attribute or manipulation where object's reaction depends on combined inputs from the collaborating users.

We address two research issues while studying manipulation on the same object's attribute. Based on the research by Basdogan et al. [5], we address the first issue in our research: the effects of using haptics on a collaborative interaction. Based on the research by Roberts et al. [6], we address the second issue in our research: the possibilities of collaboration between users from different environments.

To address the first issue, we tested the Virtual Dollhouse application of different versions: without haptics functionality and with haptics functionality, to be compared. As suggested by Kim et al. [7], we also test this comparison over Internet, not just over LAN. To address the second issue, we test the Virtual Dollhouse application between user of non-immersive display and immersive display environments. We analyze the usefulness of immersive display environment as suggested by Otto et al.[8], as they said that it holds the key for effective remote collaboration.

This paper is organized as follows: Section 2 explains the collaboration taxonomy and demo scenario; Section 3 describes the implementation; Section 4 shows testing results and discussions; Finally, Section 5 concludes and identifies future works of this research.

2 Collaboration Taxonomy and Demo Scenario

2.1 Taxonomy of Collaboration

The taxonomy, as in Fig. 1, starts with a category of objects: manipulation of distinct objects and same object. In many CVE applications [2] users collaborate by manipulating distinct objects. For manipulating the same object, sequential manipulation also exists in many CVE applications. For example, in a CVE scene, each user moves one object, and then they take turn in moving the other objects.

Concurrent manipulation of objects has been demonstrated in related work [3] by moving a heavy object together. In concurrent manipulation of objects, users can manipulate in category of attributes: same attribute or distinct attributes.

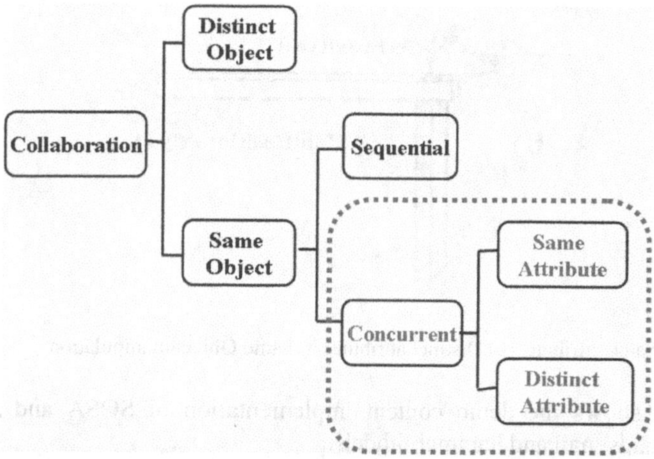

Fig. 1. Taxonomy of collaboration

2.2 Demo Scenario – Virtual Dollhouse

We construct Virtual Dollhouse application in order to demonstrate concurrent object manipulation. Concurrent manipulation is when more than one user wants to manipulate the object together, e.g. lifting a block together. The users were presented with several building blocks, a hammer, and several nails. In this application, two users have to work together to build a doll house.

The scenario for the first collaboration case is when two users want to move a building block together, so that both of them need to manipulate the "position" attribute of the block, as seen in Fig. 2(a). We call this case as SOSA (Same Object Same Attribute). The scenario for the second collaboration case is when one user is holding a building block (keep the "position" attribute to be constant) and the other is fixing the block to another block (set the "set fixed" or "release from gravity" attribute to be true), as seen in Fig. 2(b). We call this case as SODA (Same Object Different Attribute).

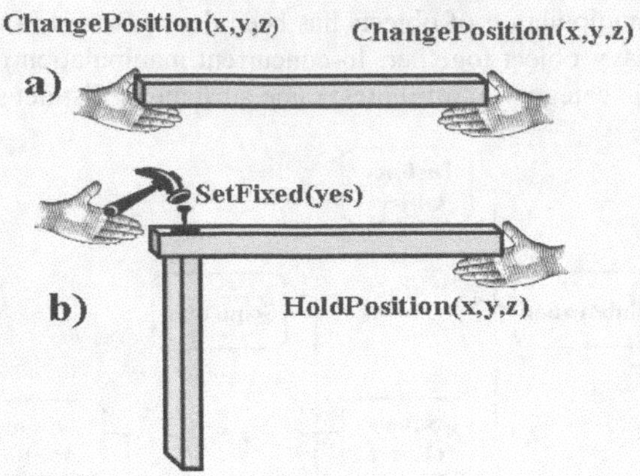

Fig. 2. (a) Same attribute, (b) Distinct attributes in Same Object manipulation

Fig. 3 shows the demo content implementation of SOSA and SODA with blocks, hands, nail and hammer models.

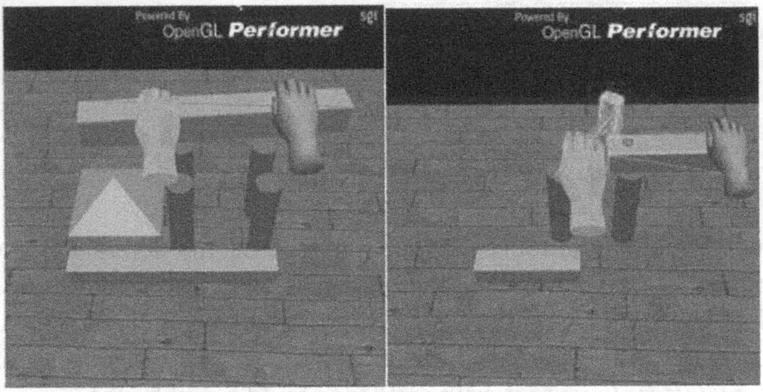

Fig. 3. Demo content implementation

3 Implementation

3.1 System Implementation

A 2D map is the basis of our algorithm because an accurate 2D map could build an accurate 3D model. SGI OpenGL Performer [9] is used in implementing this application. The application is programmed in C/C++ language in Microsoft Windows environment. A force-feedback interaction device is attached to each collaborating computer. The interaction devices were configured to support at least 3 degrees of freedom (DOF), which includes front-back, left-right, up-down movements. VRPN [10] server is executed to provide management of networked interaction devices to work with the VR application.

We use NAVERLib [11], a middleware used for managing several VR tasks such as device and network connections, events management, specific modeling, shared state management, etc. We use nvmDisplayManager to enable same display views in more than one computer. The module nvmDeviceManager is used for managing communications to VRPN servers attached by interaction devices. nvmEventManager is used to enable events sending from devices to system, and vice versa. nvmDSSM (dynamic shared state management) [12] is used to implement shared-state management used in networked physics engine.

The physics engine in our implementation is an adaptation of AGEIA PhysX SDK [13] to work with SGI OpenGL Performer's space and coordinate systems. This physics engine has a shared-state management so that two collaborating computers can have identical physics simulation states. Using this physics engine, object's velocity during interaction can be captured to be sent as force-feedbacks to the hands that are grabbing the objects.

Fig. 4 shows system architecture of the implementation.

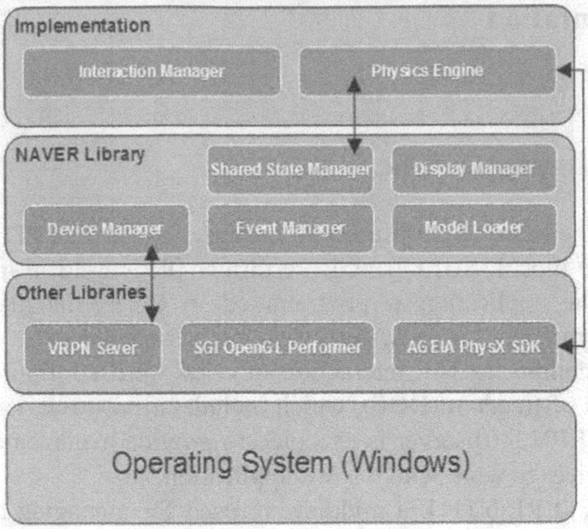

Fig. 4. System architecture collaboration in different immersion

3.2 System Implementation

Each user has an input device attached to one computer. For implementation between the same display environments, two PCs are used for testing, where each PC has a force-feedback joystick attached. For implementation between non-immersive and immersive display environments, the test-bed consists of one PC and one CAVE [14] system. In the CAVE system, the input device used is SPIDAR [15] for movements and wand for selecting/object grabbing button.

The test subjects for each of LAN, Internet, and PC-CAVE collaboration were two female adults of age 20s. Before testing, both users were trained previously on how to use the input devices. However, one user was more trained than the other, so that this user was the one to conduct voice commands during the collaboration (be the collaboration leader).

Fig. 5 shows overview of user test issues addressed by this paper on network collaborative interaction in different immersion. The comparisons were done with SOSA demo content shown in Fig. 3(a).

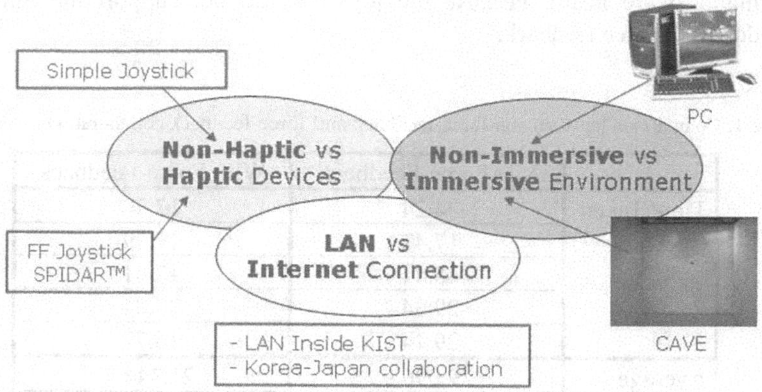

Fig. 5. Overview of comparative study in different immersion

4 Experimental Result and Review

4.1 Non-Haptics and Haptics Collaboration over LAN

The simple interaction scenarios without force feedback were done quite well over LAN. The physics simulation done over LAN was also successfully synchronized. The physics simulation on both computers showed identical objects positions and orientations at all time.

For the SOSA case, there was no problem when there were two hands having the same joystick push (same device driver's values). After configuration in XML file, collaboration leader can be the stronger hand than the other. This can avoid contradiction when the two users try to move to opposite directions.

The force-feedback functionality impressed users in the way that they could sense it when their partner moved to certain directions (two axes: left-right and forward-backward). With this force feedback, users immediately followed each other's movements. Therefore, no configuration of "which hand is stronger" needed in the XML file. It gave a sense of natural collaboration between users.

When the time taken to lift a single block was measured, it can be seen from Table 1 that users collaborated more quickly than using no force feedback. During the collaboration, users also used less voice commands ("go left!", "go forward!") compared to using no force feedback. Only "go up!" and "go down!" voice commands were heard, because the joysticks do not support the third axis (up-down) of force feedback.

Table 1. Comparison between non-force-feedback and force-feedback collaboration

	Non Force-Feedback	With Force-Feedback
Time Taken (seconds)	24.24	17.26
	17.42	17.29
	45.44	17.61
	29.34	37.84
	29.14	16.72
Average	29.096 s	21.344 s

4.2 Non-Haptics and Haptics Collaboration over Internet

Because of voice clarity problems, we did not use voice communication during the collaboration over Internet. However, users could still follow the color codes of the block to be grabbed as guidance, thus following their natural reflexes without waiting for voice commands.

The comparison between using force-feedback and no force-feedback showed similar results to the collaboration over LAN, as seen in Table 2. Force-feedback functionality was considered helpful in sensing the collaboration partner's presence.

Table 2. Comparison between force-feedback and non-force-feedback collaboration over Internet

	Non Force-Feedback	With Force-Feedback
Time Taken (seconds)	40.11	47.28
	40.34	32.34
	31.95	29.92
	52.35	38.81
	52.98	36.27
Average	43.55 s	36.92 s

During the non-haptic collaboration over Internet, there were no problems felt by users. However, the haptic collaboration was distracted by network delays. The force feedback was a bit late to be felt, compared to the display of the object's movements (visual feedback). It was also not smooth (more jerking), because the small values of the force feedback might have been lost in network.

4.3 Collaboration between Non-Immersive and Immersive Display Environments

We test the SOSA algorithm between PC and CAVE system over LAN. For the non-haptic collaboration, we disable the force-feedback functionalities of the input devices: SPIDAR (attached to CAVE) and joystick. With no force-feedback, it was very difficult to control collaboration, because of the nature of the input devices that caused difference in hand's speeds between SPIDAR and joystick. SPIDAR is a tracker type device, where absolute positions are taken for hand movements. Joystick is an analog type device, where velocity values are taken for hand movements. CAVE user could move the SPIDAR to any place inside CAVE so quickly (which is mapped to movements inside the CAVE) so that the PC user could not follow the movements with joystick.

For the haptic collaboration, we enabled the force-feedback functionalities of the input devices, especially SPIDAR that has 3 axes of force-feedback support compared to only 2 axes in joystick. SPIDAR movement is more controlled because of resulting force feedback from the collaboration with the partner. The force prevented SPIDAR to move too quickly to any locations inside the CAVE.

Users thought that it is more intuitive to use SPIDAR than joystick for the purpose of manipulating the objects. This is explainable, because SPIDAR's movements by hand can map directly to object's movements inside the VE. Joystick is more intuitive for simulations that require velocity-driven movements, such as driving or flight simulations.

Moreover, users also thought that immersive display is useful to make a feeling of real-world manipulation of the object, compared to desktop display. A feeling of moving a heavy object was perceived as more real by users. Table 4 summarizes five experiments results for total comparison.

Table 3. Network collaboration b/w PC-CAVE with force-feedback over LAN

	With Force-Feedback
Time Taken (seconds)	20.33
	15.81
	16.44
	10.76
	20.04
Average	16.676 s

Table 4. Comparison of network collaborative interaction in different immersion and different network environment

	PC-PC Non Force-Feedback	PC-PC Force-Feedback	CAVE-PC Force-Feedback
LAN	29.096	21.344	16.676 s
Internet	43.55	36.92	-

5 Conclusion

We have implemented an application for CVE based on VR systems and simulation of physics law. The system allows reconfiguration of the simulation elements so that users can see the effects of the different configurations. The network support enables users from different places to work together when interacting with the simulation, and see each other's simulation results.

From our series of testing of the application over different networks and environments, we can conclude that the use of haptics functionality (force-feedback device) is useful for users to feel each other's presence. It also helps collaboration to be performed more effectively (no time wasted). However, network delays caused problems on the haptics smoothness. In the future, we will update our algorithm by studying the possible solutions like indicated by Glencross et al. [16].

We also conclude that the use of tracker-type input device like SPIDAR is more intuitive for a task where users are faced with a set of objects to select and manipulate. From the display view of point, immersive display environment is more suitable for simulation of dealing with object manipulation that requires force and weight feeling, compared to non-immersive display environment such as PC.

Acknowledgement. This work was supported by Korea Institute of Science and Technology (KIST) through the Tangible Space Initiative Project.

References

1. Margery, D., Arnaldi, B., Plouzeau, N.: A General Framework for Cooperative Manipulation in Virtual Environments. In: 5th Eurographics Workshop on Virtual Environments. Vienna (1999)

2. Johnson, A., Roussos, M., Leigh, J.: The NICE Project: Learning Together in a Virtual World. In: IEEE Virtual Reality Annual International Symposium (VRAIS 98). Atlanta (1998)
3. Wolff, R., Roberts, D.J., Otto, O.: A Study of Event Traffic during the Shared Manipulation of Objects within a Collaborative Virtual Environment. In: Presence, vol. 13, no. 3, pp. 251-262 (June 2004)
4. Ruddle, R.A., Savage, J.C.D., Jones, D.M.: Symmetric and Asymmetric Action Integration During Cooperative Object Manipulation in Virtual Environments. In: ACM Transactions on Computer-Human Interaction, vol. 9, no. 4 (Dec. 2002)
5. Basdogan, C., Ho, C., Srinivasan, M.A., Slater, M.:An Experimental Study on the Role of Touch in Shared Virtual Environments. In: ACM Transactions on Computer Human Interaction, vol. 7, no. 4, pp. 443-460 (Dec. 2000)
6. Roberts, D., Wolff, R., Otto, O.: Supporting a Closely Coupled Task between a Distributed Team: Using Immersive Virtual Reality Technology. In: Computing and Informatics, vol. 24, no. 1 (2005)
7. Kim, J., Kim, H., Tay, B.K., Muniyandi, M., Srinivasan, M.A., Jordan, J., Mortensen, J., Oliveira, M., Slater, M.: Transatlantic touch: A study of haptic collaboration over long distance. In: Presence: Teleoperator and Virtual Environments, vol. 13, no. 3, pp. 328-337 (2004)
8. Otto, O., Roberts, D., Wolff, R.: A Review on Effective Closely-Coupled Collaboration using Immersive CVE's. In: Proceedings of ACM VRCIA. Hong Kong (June 2006)
9. Silicon Graphics Inc., "OpenGL Performer," http://www.sgi.com/products/software/performer/ (2005)
10. Taylor, R. M., Hudson, T. C., Seeger, A., Weber, H., Juliano, J., Helser, A.T.: VRPN: A device-independent, network-transparent VR peripheral system. In: ACM International Symposium on Virtual Reality Software and Technology (VRST 2001). Berkeley (2001)
11. Park, C., Ko, H.D., Kim, T.: NAVER: Networked and Augmented Virtual Environment aRchitecture; design and implementation of VR framework for Gyeongju VR Theater. In: Computers & Graphics, vol. 27, pp. 223-230 (2003)
12. Park, Y., Kim, J., Ko, H., Choy, Y.: Dynamic Shared State Management For Distributed Interactive Virtual Environment. In: Proceedings of International Conference on Artificial Reality and Telexistence (ICAT 2004). Seoul (2004)
13. AGEIA: AGEIA PhysX SDK, http://www.ageia.com
14. Cruz-Neira, C., Sandin, D. J., DeFanti, T. A., Kenyon, R.V., Hart, J.C.: The CAVE: audio visual experience automatic virtual environment. In: Communications of the ACM, vol. 35, issue 6, pp. 64-72 (1992)
15. Sato, M.: Development of string-based force display. In: Proceedings of the Eighth International Conference on Virtual Reality and Multimedia, Workshop 2. Gyeongju (2002)
16. Glencross, M., Jay, C., Feasel, J., Kohli, L., Whitton, M.: Effective Cooperative Haptic Interaction over the Internet. In: Proceedings of IEEE Virtual Reality Conference 2007. Charlotte (2007)

Protein-Protein Interaction Network and Gene Ontology

Yunkyu Choi, Seok Kim, Gwan-Su Yi and Jinah Park

Information and Communications University (ICU) 119,
Munjiro, Yusong-gu, Daejeon, 305-732 South Korea

{20062530, gstone0103, gsyi, jinah} @icu.ac.kr

Abstract Evolution of computer technologies makes it possible to access a large amount and various kinds of biological data via internet such as DNA sequences, proteomics data and information discovered about them. It is expected that the combination of various data could help researchers find further knowledge about them. Roles of a visualization system are to invoke human abilities to integrate information and to recognize certain patterns in the data. Thus, when the various kinds of data are examined and analyzed manually, an effective visualization system is an essential part. One instance of these integrated visualizations can be combination of protein-protein interaction (PPI) data and Gene Ontology (GO) which could help enhance the analysis of PPI network. We introduce a simple but comprehensive visualization system that integrates GO and PPI data where GO and PPI graphs are visualized side-by-side and supports quick reference functions between them. Furthermore, the proposed system provides several interactive visualization methods for efficiently analyzing the PPI network and GO directed-acyclic-graph such as context-based browsing and common ancestors finding.,

1 Introduction

Gene Ontology (GO) represents a set of concepts within three independent domains (biological process, molecular function and cellular component) and organizes the concepts in a hierarchical way based on the relationships among the concepts. GO describes the gene products such that it may be used to reason about the gene products and their relations. Protein-protein interaction (PPI) data is already very large, yet still evolving in that there are many unknown interactions to be discovered, understood and verified. For successful analysis of a PPI network, the GO is often referred to infer some properties of certain proteins in question. Thanks to the evolution of internet technologies and biologists'

O.-H. Byeon et al. (eds.), *Future Application and Middleware Technology on e-Science*,
DOI 10.1007/978-1-4419-1719-5_16,

commitment, these data are openly shared via internet. However, to reach and get higher level of knowledge about biology, it is necessary to integrate various kinds of data from various sources, such as GO and PPI. Since such an integrated analysis process is highly interactive, having user-friendly interface integrating both PPI and GO will influence profitable outputs. Visualization systems are the key to the interface, if they can provide an environment where the user can easily integrate information. In this paper, we introduce a simple yet comprehensive visualization system that displays PPI and GO graphs side-by-side and that supports cross-referencing functions between them. We dubbed our system as PINGO (Protein-protein Interaction aNd Gene Ontology). In the following sections, related works, the PINGO system implementation, case study and discussion will be described in detail.

2 Related works

Although there are many researches utilizing GO for PPI analysis, there are only a few systems that provide visual interface to the integration. Table 1 summarizes the comparisons of existing visualization systems regarding combined aspects of GO and PPI information.

Table 1. Comparisons in cross-referencing aspects

	PINGO	BiNGO	APID2NET	Osprey
Available graphic viewers	PPI and GO viewers	PPI and GO viewers	PPI viewer only	PPI viewer only
Dynamic updates between the viewers	Dynamic update	Require manual loading	N/A	N/A
Communication between GO and PPI database	List view with color marking; Tab list of related terms going from PPI to GO, as well as from GO to PPI	Generates new GO graph for selected proteins; Single color marking to protein with respect to selected GO	Multiple color marking on protein nodes	Multiple color marking on protein nodes

Osprey [1] visualizes PPI network whose nodes and edges represent proteins and existence of interaction between the proteins, respectively. The protein node is drawn as a disc, which is color-coded based on its related GO terms. Since there are usually more than one related GO terms, the disc is divided into sectors and each sector is colored with the solid color representing a separate GO term. It may help the user to recognize proteins of common properties, but due to the limited number of distinguishable colors, the association of a color with a GO term (or property) remains arbitrary and potentially unintuitive. More importantly, the hierarchical information of GO has lost. APID2NET [3], which uses the Cytoscape [8] framework, also employs a similar color-coding scheme of the nodes based on related GO terms. In both systems, color-coding without a separate window to display the GO graphical view is provided for the user to explore GO information. BiNGO [9] provides function to display the GO graph by selecting a set of proteins in PPI network. However, it is only a snapshot and does not provide a dynamic update capability. BiNGO highlights only proteins already displayed in the PPI network from GO reference but can add proteins to the PPI network displayed. PINGO is designed to provide easy and dynamic interaction between GO and PPI. As shown in Table 1, PINGO provides both PPI and GO views and both-way cross-reference with dynamic update between them. The details of PINGO will be explained in the following section 3.

3 Methods

To develop an efficient integrated visualization system of GO and PPI, interface, cross-reference functions and visualization methods were concerned. In terms of interface, GO and PPI are placed side-by-side with similar interface in each side. GO-to-protein(s) and protein-to-GOs cross-references are possible and each view can be dynamically updated from cross-references. To provide efficient visualization methods, we adopted context-based browsing [10], dynamic node expansion/ collapsing, LCA (Least Common Ancestor) and etc. The details of PINGO system will be explained in the following sub sections.

3.1 Overview of PINGO System

PINGO system provides easy-access interface to GO and PPI data by displaying their graphs in side-by-side manner: the left side for GO and the right side for PPI as shown in Fig. 1. The graphical views display the graphs of related data sets of the chosen IDs. To explain the interface, 'Information Tables', which are located below the 'Graphical View' windows, allow users to view grouped information in list format. On GO side, by selecting a tab, the user can examine a full GO tree, a list of chosen GO terms ('Checked GO'-tab), or a list of proteins that are associated with a selected GO term ('Related Proteins'-tab). Similarly, on PPI side, a list of proteins in the data loaded, a list of chosen proteins ('Checked Protein'-tab), or a list of related GO IDs associated with a selected protein ('Related GO'-tab). Any item can be interactively selected or deselected with a simple mouse click on the information tables as well as on the graphical windows, to navigate through the data.

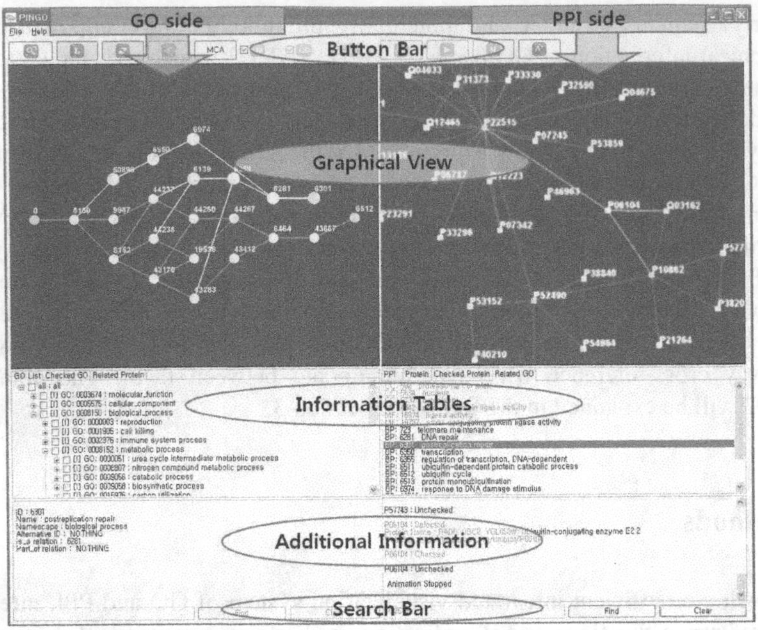

Fig. 1. PINGO system interface.

Moreover, basic design concept of the user interface is to provide similar controllability as well as the layout for both GO and PPI sides. (For instance, node in both GO and PPI sides can be selected by clicking a right mouse button.)

3.2 Details of Data

We used three kinds of data sources described in the list below.

1. Gene Ontology: OBO v1.2 format
2. Protein Interaction: MINT flat file
3. PPI-GO cross-reference: Unfiltered UniProt GO annotation @ EBI

In the list, data 1 and 3 are obtained from the Gene Ontology site (http://www.geneontology.org/) managed by The GO Consortium. These data can be accessed by remote query or downloaded as database or flat file. Remote query ensure the data up-to-dated while this requires relatively long process time caused by connection and downloading time. Data 2 is from MINT (the Molecular INTeraction database). MINT also provides data acquisition by online query and downloaded file form. Because the system should be quick and interactive for a time efficient work, downloading whole data on local system was chosen for PINGO system.

Considerations for data acquisition from internet sources are summarized in the table below.

Table 2. Comparison table for data acquisition strategy

	Run time speed	Crash	Up to dated data
Remote query	Low	Highly expected	High
Local data with auto update	High	Low probability	High
Local data with manual download	High	Low probability	Low

In Table 2 'Local data with auto update' means that before running a system checking the local data whether it is last version or not and if it is, updating it to new version. 'Crash' means program error from inconsistency of data caused by update in remote server during running time. For example, if a protein name discarded from sever while it already had been queried and used in local system, local system could not refer the removed protein from the sever; this could cause an error. Table 2 implies 'Local data with auto update' seems the best choice but this is not always possible because there should be a kind of protocols between servers and local systems for this function.

3.3 GO-PPI Cross-reference Scheme

The main feature of PINGO is the cross-reference functions between GO and PPI data. Link from a protein to GO terms makes it possible for users to infer the functions and location of the protein; the dotted arrow lines in Fig 3.2 represent this link. On the other hand, link from GO term to proteins helps users to find proteins related to concepts in which users are interested; the arrow lines in Fig 3.2 represent this link. PINGO provides these two kinds of cross-references: protein to GO terms and GO term to proteins cross-references functions. Two kinds of cross-reference are needed for the two-way cross-reference as illustrated in Fig 3.2. These two, GO to protein and protein to GO, are extracted from 'Unfiltered UniProt GO annotation @ EBI' provided by GO consortium.

To be specific, by selecting a GO term, a user can see the list of proteins that are related to the GO term and then the user can add proteins to the PPI side by selecting one of the proteins in the list. Also, the user can select a protein and access GO term list that relates to the selected protein and may add one of the GO terms in the list; proteins depicted in Fig 3.2 are UniProt proteins in MINT protein interaction data. The updated view of the cross-side is automatically refreshed. This cross-reference scheme and related data are depicted in the Fig. 2. Since this cross-reference scheme makes GO and PPI sides highly interactive, synergistic effects of GO and PPI are expected. The details of cross-reference functions are demonstrated in the section 4, case studies.

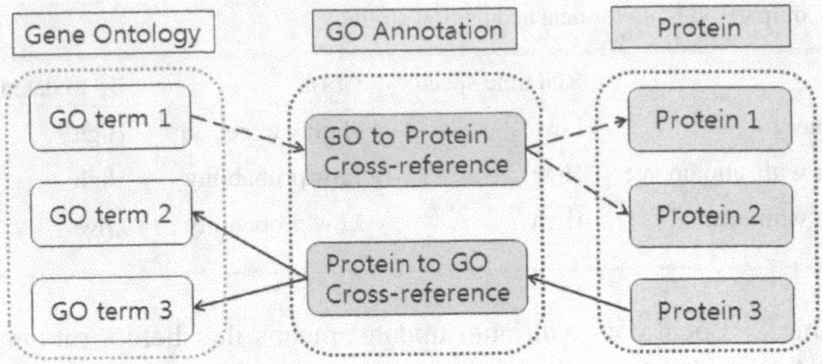

Fig. 2. The cross-reference scheme between GO and protein

3.4 Visualization Methods

3.4.1 PPI Visualization Methods

PPI network is a kind of graph that is theoretically defined as G = (V, E). PPI network is dealt as undirected graph in PINGO system. One of the biggest issues of graph visualization is the size of graph. Since the size of whole PPI network is too large (Yeast protein interaction network solely has more than 2000 proteins [7]), it is necessary to have control over the size and complexity [4, 5].

To lessen the size problem, context-based browsing mode and expansion/collapsing mode are combined. Graph is made to be interactive and layout process is animated as nodes are added or removed to enhance traceability. Force directed method [2], which provides aesthetically good layout, is employed to accommodate automatic layout of undirected relational data.

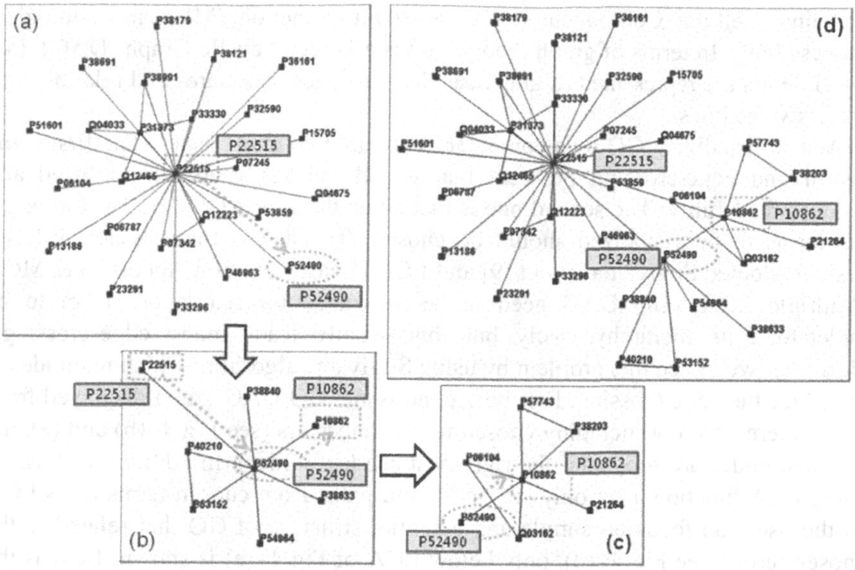

Fig. 3. Example of context-browsing, and neighbor-expansion

Context-based browsing technique, which allows expanding the network upon request to ease the tracking on what and when to look in the display, and neighbor-expansion, which allows expansion of 1st- or 2nd level neighbor of selected node, are combined for efficient navigation and examination of PPI. The Context-based browsing and neighbor-expansion details are illustrated in Fig 3. To be specific, snapshots from the top-left to bottom-right images in Fig 3.-(a), (b) and (c) demonstrate the context-based browsing navigation of network with center node position fixing. Center node of context-based browsing navigation is depicted in the following order (*P22515* → *P52490* → *P10862*). In each expansion, previously expanded connections are collapsed into a node with position freezing. As mentioned earlier, in PINGO visualization system, this PPI network can be expanded to 1st- or 2nd -level neighbors from any nodes displayed or in the 'Proteins' tab of 'Information Tables; The 1st-level expansion of three nodes (protein *P22515*, *P52490* and *P10862*) illustrated in Fig. 3-(d). Lastly, PINGO display also allows any node to be a 'sticky' node, whose position stays fixed while the positions of the other nodes are updated by the force directed display algorithm.

3.4.2 GO Visualization methods

GO provides controlled vocabularies that enable automated and computerized process of gene and gene product related concepts. GO consists of three independent domains: Cellular Component (CC), Molecular Function (MF), and Biological Process (BP). In terms of graph theory, GO is a Direct Acyclic Graph (DAG). In a DAG, terms are represented as graphical elements such as squares and relationships are drawn as lines.

When visualizing GO by a computer, there are two main issues. The first is the layout and edge-crossing problem that usually makes users be confused and reduces readability. The second one is that since the whole GO DAG is too large, the terms to be visualized should be chosen. To address these issues, PINGO system adopted Sugiyama layout [9] and LCA (Least Common Ancestor) & MCA (Multiple LCA). GO DAG need to be drawn as layered layout form to be understood its hierarchy easily but this usually leads many edge-crossings. However, we lessen this problem by using Sugiyama algorithm which main idea is to reduce the edge crossing. For the second issue, GO DAG graph displayed from chosen terms to root including chosen terms' ancestors (see Fig 4.-(b) and (e), the leftmost nodes are roots and the rightmost are leaf nodes). In addition to this, by using LCA function, user only see nodes and paths from chosen terms to its LCA so the user can focus on simple and essential structure of GO that related to the chosen terms (see Fig 4.-(d), only below LCA of Fig 4.-(e) is shown, LCA is the leftmost node). This not only simplifies the DAG but also can play a role of analysis function. Since GO categorizes concepts in hierarchical manner, finding the bifurcation term LCA can provide a clue to understand the difference and common aspects among the proteins. There may be more than one paths and therefore more than one LCA's. We compute all of them, and display as multiple LCAs that we named MCA. The detailed example will be demonstrated in the following section.

4 Case studies

In this section, example usages of PINGO system related to *Ubiquitin Cycle* will be demonstrated. For the case studies examples GO: OBO v1.2 format (June/05/2008), MINT: flat file of full species (August/04/2008), PPI-GO cross-reference: Unfiltered Uniprot GO annotation @ EBI (November/04/2008) data were used.

Suppose that we are interested in protein *P22515* and *ubiquitination.* We can start with '*P22515: UBA1, YKL210W: Ubiquitin-acivating enzyme E1*', the protein related to *ubiquitination*, can search by the protein accession ID. The chosen protein, by default, is displayed with its neighbors that interact with the protein. As shown in Fig 4.1-(a), P22515 is displayed at the center marked with (1). By opening up the 'Related GO' tab, we can examine the related GO concepts associated with the protein. Since we want to examine protein-protein interaction path that is related to ubiquitin system, we can select the GO term '*BP: 6512 Ubiquitin Cycle*' in the list: marked as (2) in Fig 4.1.

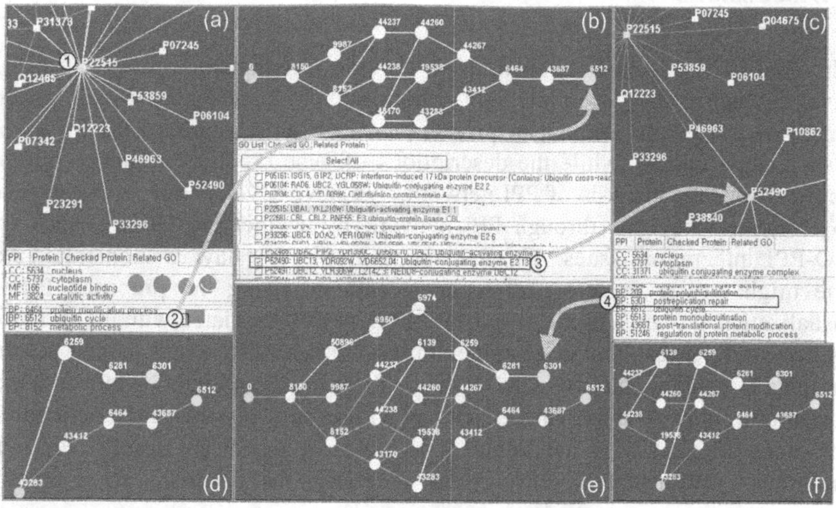

Fig. 4. Cross-reference function, LCA and MCA examples (only parts of windows are captured due to the spacing)

Then the select GO term is displayed on the GO side as shown in Fig 4.-(b), where the leftmost is the root of the GO DAG, and the rightmost is the chosen GO term. Under the 'Related Proteins' tab, all proteins related to *BP:6512* are listed. Among them, those proteins being displayed on PPI side are highlighted in the list with its corresponding colors. By examining the related protein list, we decided to look at *P52490* since its protein name is related to '*ubiquitin-conjugating enzyme E2*': marked as (3) in Fig 4.. Upon selecting it from the GO side, *P52490* in PPI side is expanded as shown in Fig 4.-(c). Now, the 'Related GO' tab lists the GO terms related to *P52490*. Under the related GO tab, we see '*BP: 6301 postreplication repair*' as well as '*BP: 6512 ubiquitin cycle*'. If we further follow the ubiquitin path, we can click on *BP:6301* in the list: marked as (4) in Fig 4.. New GO term *BP:6301* is added to GO display window as shown in Fig 4.-(e). The newly added edges are drawn in lighter-color tone. Fig 4.-(d) and (f) show two selected GO terms from the LCA and MCA, respectively. If we click on the LCA node *BP:43283*, for example, its details description including its name as "*biopolymer metabolic process*" appears in the 'Additional Information' panel under GO-side in PINGO. This example demonstrates that we were able to verify that *E1* protein and *E2* protein interacts in ubiquitin system, and this interaction pathway was found by consulting GO term '*ubiquitin cycle*'.

5 Discussions

The goal of visualization systems is to provide insights from the given data by invoking human abilities to integrate information and to recognize certain patterns in the data. The vast amount of protein-protein interaction data calls for a good visualization system, while the descriptions of gene products in Gene Ontology help enhance the analysis of PPI network. We have developed a simple interface to effectively navigate through PPI network by augmenting GO interface with GO-PPI integration issues. Through the example, we have demonstrated how one might utilize the cross-referencing features. Using the proposed PINGO visualization system, a user can see the PPI network associated with the GO terms by cross-references, he can examine similarities and differences among selected proteins by looking into its LCA/MCA graph of the associated GO terms. We are currently working on improving PINGO by adding more features and functionalities for more efficient work environment to produce significant results. From the preliminary evaluation of PINGO, we identified the following three areas of improvements.

Firstly, automatic data updating from various data source without conflict should be studied carefully. After this establishes a firm and stable base of integration of data, we could utilize integration of up-to-dated ontology and PPI data. As for an example of integration, a user can queries by combining GO and PPI like 'Find all proteins related to *ubiquitin cycle* and interact with proteins related with *postreplication repair*'

Secondly, although a user can check intersection set of GO related proteins and PPI network, it is difficult to know which GO terms linked with which proteins without selecting GO term and read the related protein list. One possible solution for this problem is to group proteins by related GO terms on PPI graphical view. Another potential solution which is already explored in Osprey and APID2NET is to use color-coding scheme. But as pointed in the earlier section, it may suffer from its own limitation: When many GO terms or proteins related color coding, it is hard to understand their relations to GO terms because of similar colors.

Lastly, GO has three different categories (CC: cellular component, MF: molecular function and BP: biological process) that should be treated differently, specializing their own characteristics. For example, directly associating GO terms in CC with a protein node seems reasonable but not for those under MF and BP. Since the function concepts in MF and process concepts in BP involves more than one object, it seems more reasonable to associate GO terms to the edges in PPI.

Acknowledgments This work was supported by grant No. R01-2005-000-10824-0 from the Basic Research Program of the Korea Science & Engineering Foundation.

References

1. Breitkreutz Bobby-Joe, Stark Chris, Tyers Mike (2003) Osprey: a network visualization system. Genome biol. 4(3):22
2. Eades P (1984) A Heuristic for Graph Drawing. congr. Numerantium 42:149-160
3. Hernandez-Toro Juan, Prieto Carlos, De Las Rivas Javier (2007) APID2NET: unified interactome graphic analyzer. Bioinformatics 23(18): 2495–2497
4. Herman Ivan, Melançon Guy, Marshall M Scott (2000) Graph Visualization and Navigation in Information Visualization: A Survey. IEEE trans. on vis. and comput. graph. 6(1):24-43
5. Kershenbaum Aaron, Murray Keitha (2005) Visualization of network structures. J. of comput. sci. in coll. 21(2):59-71
6. Maere Steven, Heymans Karel, Kuiper Martin (2005) BiNGO: a Cytoscape plugin to assess overrepresentation of Gene Ontology categories in Biological Networks. Bioinformatics 21(16):3448–3449
7. Schwikowski Benno, Uetz Peter, Fields Stanley (2000) A network of protein–protein interactions in yeast. nat. biotecnol. 18:1257–1261
8. Shannon Paul, Markiel Andrew, Ozier Owen, Baliga Nitin S, Wang Jonathan T, Ramage Daniel, Amin Nada, Schwikowski Benno, Ideker Trey (2003) Cytoscape: A Software Environment for Integrated Models of Biomolecular Interaction Networks. Genome res. 13:2498–2504
9. Sugiyama K, Tagawa S, Toda M (1981) Methods for Visual Understanding of Hierarchical System Structures. IEEE trans. on syst. Man and cybern. 11(2):109-125
10. Tzitzikas Yannis, Hainaut JeanLuc (2006) On the Visualization of Large sized Ontologies. proc. of the work. conf. on adv. vis. Interfaces